ESSENTIAL LIFE SKILLS FOR TWEENS

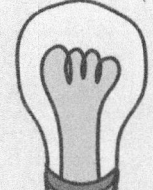

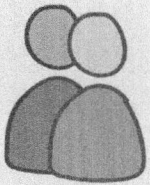

Tips and Advice for Developing Independence, Self-Awareness and Positive Relationships

Copyright © 2023 – Noah Donegan

All rights reserved.

It is not legal to reproduce, duplicate, or transmit any part of this document in either electronic means or printed format. Recording of this publication is strictly prohibited and any storage of this document is not allowed unless with written permission from the publisher except for the use of brief quotations in a book review.

Disclaimer

The information provided in this book is intended for general informational purposes only and should not be construed as professional advice. Although every effort has been made to ensure its accuracy and completeness, the author makes no guarantees or warranties about the content. Readers seeking medical advice should consult with a licensed healthcare provider before acting on any information contained herein. Similarly, readers seeking financial advice should consult with a qualified financial advisor before making any significant decisions related to their finances. By using the information provided in this book, the reader agrees to assume full responsibility and risk associated with their use, and releases the author from any liability for any direct or indirect damages or losses resulting from the use of such information.

Table of Contents

Introduction 8

Chapter 1: Definition of "Tween" and the Importance of Life Skills 10

    The Definition of "Tween" 11

    Life Skills and Why Do We Talk About Them 12

    The Impact of Life Skills on Academic and Personal Success 14

    Academic Skills 15

Chapter 2: Social Skills 18

    Effective Communication 19

    Conflict Resolution 22

        Exhibits of Conflict 23

        How to Avoid and/or Resolve Conflict 25

    Empathy and Understanding Others 27

        How to Show Empathy Towards Others 28

    Positive Relationships 30

    Cultural Sensitivity 32

Chapter 3: Self-Esteem and Self-awareness 34

    Identifying and Managing Emotions 35

    What to Do When Everything Feels Like It's Too Much 38

    Self-Awareness 40

    Body and Mental Health 42

    Mens Sana in Corpore Sano 43

Chapter 4: Decision-Making and Problem-Solving 45

    Understanding the Decision-Making Process 47

        The Definition 48

The Steps 49
Informed Decisions are the Best Decisions 50
Generating Ideas and Creative 51
Problem-Solving 51
The Definition 52
Creating Creative Credible Solutions 53
Why is Creative Problem-Solving so Important? 55
Critical Thinking and Analysis 56
The Definition 57
Some Advice to Improve Your Critical Thinking 58
What Would I Need Critical Thinking For? 59

Chapter 5: Practical Skills for Daily Life 61
Time-Planning and Management 62
Why Should You Learn to Manage Your Time 64
Tips for Time-Planning 65
Some Tools for Time-Management 67
Budgeting and Money-Management 68
What Do I Need to Know About Money-Management? 69
Cooking and Meal Preparation 73
Basic Cooking Skills and Techniques 75
How to Prep a Meal 77
Safety first! 79
House Responsibilities 80
How Can I Help? – Personal Space Edition 81
How Can I Help? – Common Area Edition 83
Tips for House Cleaning 84

Chapter 6: Preparation for the Future 86

Why is This Topic So Important? 87

   Tips for Career Searching 88

   Tools for Career Searching 90

Leadership and Teamwork Skills 91

   Tips for Leadership and Teamwork Skills 92

   The Benefits of Teamwork 94

Chapter 7: Health and Wellness 96

Healthy Eating Habits 97

   Tips for Healthier Eating Habits 98

Physical Exercise 100

   Tips for Introducing Sports and Exercises into your Habits 101

Sleep Hygiene and Mental Health 103

   Why is Sleeping So Important? 104

   Strategies for Introducing Good Sleeping Habits in Your Life ... 105

Environmental Awareness and Sustainability 107

   How to Help the Environment 108

Chapter 8: Digital Skills 110

How to be Safe and Responsible on the Internet 111

   Online Safety Tips and Guidelines 113

   Cyberbullying and Social-Media 115

Fake News and Online Scams 116

   Tips on How to Identify and Protect Yourself from Fake News and Online Scams 117

How to Do Research Online 118

Chapter 9: Creative and Artistic Skills 121

Expressing Yourself Through Art and Creativity 122

   How to Explore Different Art Forms and Our Own Creativity 123

Some of the Different Art Forms that Exist 125
Developing Talents and Interests 127
Chapter 10: Cultural and Global Awareness 129
Understanding and Respecting Cultural Differences 130
A Broad Perspective of the World 133
Diversity and Inclusion 134
Conclusion.. 135

Introduction

Hi! Welcome to my book!

We're going to go on a wonderful trip together: we are going to explore the future of what may come and travel together through all the emotions and doubts you may have about all sorts of things. We are going to talk about them and discuss the tips and tricks that you already have up your sleeve and that you may not know about yet.

I have been a tween myself and let me tell you: I struggled. In hindsight, the main problem with my personal upbringing, especially during your age, is that no one had really sat me down and prepared me, not even to clear my thoughts. Most people think that the teenage years are the most difficult ones for a young person, but sometimes it's what came before that paves the way. Think of it this way: life isn't always easy, most of the hardships don't come with a manual and you might feel lost and confused. Life is also amazing, surprising and full of exciting adventures! It's worth it.

Anyways, back to my own upbringing: I think that, as someone that has experienced the difficulties of being that age and having to learn most of the stuff one needs to know on my own, a book like this might have come in handy.

I put in the word, you put in the work: how does that sound?

Remember that you can always come back to this book anytime you want, I'm always going to be here to give the piece of advice you may need.

We are going to talk about so much stuff together, especially emotions, relationships but also money management, health, how to approach world problems and how to control negative feelings. How to make thoughtful decisions and how to think about your own future without panicking.

It's going to be great. I promise.

So, shall we start?

Chapter 1: Definition of "Tween" and the Importance of Life Skills

Let's start with the right foot: the first thing on the agenda is to understand what are you going through in the most complete way.

Defining an aspect of your life by the age group you fall into might seem limiting, but it's a good way to start this journey: by reminding yourself that you aren't alone in this. At all. Trust me when I tell you that most of the troubles you may feel embarrassed to not being able to handle, most of the thoughts you might not feel ready to talk about, are shared experiences amongst people who are in the same age group as you are. Sometimes, it doesn't hurt to feel less alone. Age related issues or common experiences don't necessarily revolve around tween and teenage years: people in their 20s, 30s, 40s, 50s and even later in life have a higher chance of being able to share the same considerations and reflections about life.

As we established that starting off with the right foot is half the work done, you might ask me: why do I need to start caring about my life skills right now?

You may feel like you are too young to care about certain topics and let me reassure you that this won't take you away from your own hobbies and interests. This is more about being the most prepared you can be for what's to come.

Say, for example, that you decide to put aside the topic of money-management for when you think you will need it more: you will be at the age you decided to put these thoughts aside to, and you won't even know how to approach the subject or how to even start handling money!

That's why you need solid foundations, so that when the time is right, you will be ready.

The Definition of "Tween"

So, let's dive into the definition of this term.

It typically refers to the period in your life that starts at around 9 years old and end at about 12. The ages we are referring to are not at all definite and can change, but these are the general limits of when it starts and when it ends. The term itself generates from the word "between", because these are the years that pass *between* childhood and adolescence. At 8 years old you are still a child, whereas at 13, hence the "teen" in the number, you start your teenage years that end once you hit the 19 years old mark.

It's very interesting to note that Tolkien, the author of the Lord of the Rings and the Hobbit, actually used the word "tween" for describing hobbits that were in their twenties and that were quite the troublemakers, as hobbits hit adulthood in their early 30s. However, this is not the reason why this term has become popular.

As already mentioned, it is most probable that the word itself is a derivative of the word "between", but the popularization of this term is to be found in the early 1990s and was first referred to the age group that goes from 8 to 15 years of age.

Besides, there are many different alternatives of the word "tween", the most common ones being "preteen" and "preadolescent". Another term you could encounter is "middle-schooler", but all of these are not quite as accurate as "tween": "preteen" implies that the main point of this age group is the arrival of adolescence, which is true, but at the same time it limits our view on the fact that the end of the childhood years plays a big part; "middle-schooler" might also be correct, but it doesn't all come down to which school you might be attending or preparing to attend, does it?

So, "tween" is the word we are looking for. You are literally in between your childhood and your teenage years. Things are changing both in you and outside you. You may feel like you are starting to grow and become another older version of yourself.

Again, not everyone talks about how challenging and crucial these next few years are going to be, but we are here just for this reason.

Life Skills and Why Do We Talk About Them

The real question is "why do we talk about them during these few years?"

Apart from what was previously mentioned in the introduction of this chapter, it is crucial to understand that this is the time in which you could start defining what the rest of your life could look like, at least for the next few years.

See, if we start actually understanding what your abilities are right now, what you're interested in and how we could develop your skills into proper studies and goals, you are going to be so relieved once it is the actual time to choose.

I know it might feel far away from your life right now, but remember that if you do it now, you might have the chance not to do it later!

It's not even only about your interests: with "life skills" we are also referring to how to safely surf the internet, how to manage your money, how to interact with other people, how to acquire or develop leadership skills... anything that can help you take off from your childhood years and be as ready as possible for what's to come.

This is the best time to do so, because your brain is now developing differently and much faster than it was years ago, you are ready to learn some more and you are most definitely becoming your own person, I understand that it is both scary and exciting.

Think of it this way: imagine yourself as a house. Whatever type of house you want, let your creativity run wild. Only problem is, that you don't actually exist... yet.

This is because the ground you are building your house on isn't really ready, it is still wild, with tall grass and mud all around. What you need to do is to work the ground and lay the actual foundations of the house, meaning for yourself! Without them, you could build the floor and even some rooms, but the probability of them being unstable and falling is very high.

You have to literally build yourself from the ground up!

The Impact of Life Skills on Academic and Personal Success

School is very important and it's going to be for the time to come. Elementary school is usually a bit lighter, at least in terms of homework load and subjects to study.

There's a chance that you are already attending middle school, or maybe you haven't started it yet. A lot of things are going to change, and because of that, it's best if you start approaching this new chapter right away.

By learning how to study properly, how to organize your time in the most efficient way and be satisfied with your own preparation, you will be able to have a clearer view of your surroundings and you'll still be able to have your own personal time to do what you want, to look for new interests or to relax.

Going to middle school is also a time of great change relationship-wise. You might need a whole new set of skills in order to interact with others, both with kids your age and with the adults in your life, whether we are talking about professors or adult family members.

This doesn't imply that you didn't know how to interact with others or that you didn't know what you were doing in elementary school, it just means that this new chapter might be challenging and that you need new skills to approach it. It's kind of like when any technological device needs an upgrade. It has to shut down and learn new "skills" in order to work correctly as the new upgraded version. You of course don't need to shut down, quite the opposite, but you need some time to adjust to this new reality.

It's completely normal and necessary, having to live through all of these phases in order to learn and grow.

Academic Skills

Let's now dive into the actual tips and learning methods you can apply on your day-to-day studying habits.

First thing first, you should try and pinpoint what you think your difficulties are and what you want to improve.

Here are some of the most common ones:

- **Disorganization** ⇨ This can be happening for many different reasons, what you can do to improve your organization is to **plan ahead**. For example, try and use a planning device (it can be an app or just a sheet of paper) and create a chart where you put the days of the week divided by day and hour (you can purchase an agenda as well if you want). The next step would be to **write down** every single task, homework you have to do or event you need to attend. Put the hours you stay at school and the hours you spend at home. Don't forget to leave room for personal time in there. This can be an excellent start to the betterment of your organization.

- **Distractions** ⇨ This is a big one, most of the students, even way older ones, might have some trouble with **staying focused**. The first thing to do would be to find, if possible, the **perfect spot** for you to study. It can be in the kitchen, in a school study room, in your own room, on a desk... the choices are more than you think! After finding the perfect spot, you need to understand what's best for you between **studying with someone** or by yourself. If **silence and isolation** make you more focused, then you could try and use a pair of headphones to reduce outside noises and dive in. Both of the things can be a choice too: for example, you prefer studying History by yourself but you'd prefer to study Math with a group of friends or with a family member. Try and be as **objective** as possible, make choices depending on what you think would be best for you and not necessarily what can be more fun, because there can be many other situations where the main focus is to have fun, but this is not one of them. There's nothing wrong with having fun while studying, quite the opposite actually, but fun shouldn't be the priority whilst trying to avoid distractions. Finally, once you are seated at the right spot with or without company, **clear the space around you**. Turn off the music if your brain keeps wanting to focus on it (if you need sounds whilst listening, there are great playlists out there that were created specifically for this reason), clear the desk or whatever surface you're using of any distractions such as toys, phones, charms and so on. Sometimes, studying for a long time is counter-productive, because our brain gets too tired and focusing seems impossible: **take small (5-10 minutes) breaks** whenever you feel a bit too overwhelmed, turn off your brain and then turn it on again.

- **Forgetfulness** ⇨Sometimes we do everything right but the new information we just studied doesn't stick in our brain. This doesn't mean anything. Maybe you just need to change studying techniques. There are many, for example **color coding and post-it notes** can be very helpful, especially if you have a photographic memory. **Recording yourself** while trying to explain what you're studying at the moment is as good as doing the same thing but **in front of a mirror**. These techniques can help you memorize the way you say certain sentences and can make you a better judge on your quality of studying, as well as memorizing what you need to in a much faster way.

Underlining and schematizing notes and pages is incredibly helpful and it would be best if done on paper with a pen, because while writing, your brain automatically absorbs the information you are putting on paper, so it's like having half the job already done. If you still have trouble remembering, maybe **express your concerns to a family member or a teacher**. Remember that having trouble focusing or remembering things doesn't make you stupid or less of.

- **Anxiety and Expectations** ⇨ There's something really important we need to talk about. Your life is your own, not someone else's. It is yours and your happiness and mental health must be your number one priority, always. Your own expectations are the ones that matter, and you should be happy with whatever outcome you have, as long as you think you have done everything you could have. I know that sometimes, school makes people anxious and stressed, and it's understandable. But believe me when I say that **your satisfaction with your own work is the most important thing**.

Chapter 2: Social Skills

LISTEN ACTIVELY
WHEN SOMEONE IS SPEAKING, REALLY TRY TO LISTEN AND UNDERSTAND WHAT THEY'RE SAYING.

REPEAT BACK WHAT YOU'VE HEARD
THIS SHOWS THAT YOU WERE LISTENING AND HELPED TO CLARIFY ANY MISUNDERSTANDINGS.

ASK QUESTIONS
IF YOU'RE NOT SURE ABOUT SOMETHING, ASK FOR CLARIFICATION.

USE NONVERBAL CUES
FACIAL EXPRESSIONS, EYE CONTACT, AND BODY LANGUAGE CAN ALL AFFECT HOW WELL YOU COMMUNICATE.

BE AWARE OF YOUR OWN COMMUNICATION STYLE
WE ALL HAVE DIFFERENT WAYS OF COMMUNICATING, SO BE AWARE OF HOW YOU COME ACROSS TO OTHERS.

Life is changing, you are changing, everything is new and exciting. There are some things that can be quite scary though, right? For example, not everyone is a social expert that knows how to approach people and become friends, right? I certainly wasn't: before becoming a bit braver, I couldn't be described as a social butterfly. I spent many lunch-breaks on my own. Let me clarify that I didn't grow up to be a social butterfly, the difference is that I now know how to better deal with social events and have developed my set of social skills.

For me, it was more about learning how to be brave and how much bravery it would take me to approach someone I didn't know. It isn't only about being brave though: sometimes you can be more than ready, braver than ever, and still have troubles taking that step. Most of the times, it's all about your social skills more than anything else, more than being extroverted or introverted too.

Being extroverted or introverted is fine, really, either way is cool. Being or not being a social butterfly is also cool. What's not cool is if your own situation makes you uncomfortable. See, I did like spending time on my own, but I would have liked to have the option of not being alone most of my lunch-breaks, you know what I mean?

Either way, in this chapter we are going to learn a bit more about social skills, how to develop them, how to interact with others, what is empathy and why it's important, conflict resolution and so on.

Effective Communication

This is very important. The first thing to know about social skills is how to effectively communicate with your peers and in general the people in your life. Sometimes we lack a certain set of skills that help us be a bit more effortless in approaching others.

Communicating is not always easy, but there are tips you can follow to improve this skill.

- **Listening** ⇨ This is absolutely crucial. There are two different types of listening: passive listening and active listening. **Passive listening**: hearing what someone else is saying but without absorbing the information or reacting in any way. It can be very frustrating for the person that is talking, because it seems as you are not really interested in what it is said, and it can feel humiliating. **Active listening** is the opposite of the aforementioned: not only you give the person who's talking your full attention, but you are also showing signs of actually listening. For example, asking questions about the topic, nodding your head, expressively reacting to what has been said... This is the one you need to exercise, because this not only makes the other person happier, but as a result, it makes you happier. This can be very healthy and can make you fully understand the person you are talking with, whether they are talking about their own problems, their experiences or just random things. Active listening makes you a great person to have around and people will feel respected and drawn to communicate with you, because they know you are going to be listening.

- **Respect** ⇨ This can come in a few different forms, but it all comes down to how you approach the other person. You would agree that talking to a friend, to an older family member or your teacher all require different approaches, wouldn't you? This is what respect in communication is all about. You can't talk with your teacher the same way you talk to a sibling or a cousin. This is because your relation with those people is way different, and thus **requires different "languages"**. It's not that you need to selectively show respect, it's that you need to **respect everyone around you**, just in different ways.

- **Think twice** ⇨ This can also be applied to communication via phone. During a conversation, always remember to **think twice before actually saying what you think**. Try and reflect on it: am I clear headed enough? Do I really mean that? Do my words reflect my honest yet respectful opinion? Does the other person need these words from me at this moment? It's ok to not have all the answers to these questions right away, but compiling them and trying to answer them truthfully is a step further into learning to communicate. For example, if you can't understand whether you are clear minded enough to say what you want to, rather than saying it anyways you can **always take a breather and step away from the situation**. This mechanism is much easier while texting, as you're not face to face with the person you are talking to, and it's usually not a problem if it takes you a bit more to reply.

- **Body language** ⇨ There are some actual tricks you can pull by knowing how body language works. For instance, **looking someone directly in their eyes and uncrossing your arms** whilst talking to them makes the other person feel included in your space and **open to communication**. As you can imagine, smiling is always a plus, but of course this is specifically related to whomever you are talking to and in what situation you are in. For example, if an adult is scolding you, smiling could be considered disrespectful or arrogant, whether you wanted to be or not. If, however, you are talking to the same adult but this time in a calm and happy environment, smiling can do no harm. It's always better to be able to "read the room": basically, to understand the emotions of the people you are interacting with. Usually, smiling if someone is crying could make you look insensible, but if you are doing it to make a joke so that the other person could crack a smile as well, it makes you empathetic (we will talk about empathy later, don't worry)... It's always a matter of trial and error: the more you try, the more you could make mistakes, the more you can take in, and apply what you have learned to the next interaction.

Conflict Resolution

Conflicts are pretty common and normal to have. They usually happen because of clashes of interests, thoughts, different views of the same topic, and for many other reasons. The fact that they are common doesn't make them a healthy response to a tense situation.

I'm sure that you already experienced conflicts in your life. Most of the time they end up with a lot of arguing, raising voices and even physical altercations. Nearly all conflicts that happen this way end up not actually resolving the rooted issue, but rather intensifying it. It can lead to damaged relationships and even the ending of some of them.

Life-long friendships that are suddenly torn apart, groups of people that can't stand each other, family members that can't stay in the same room as one another. It's sad, especially if situations could have been handled in different, healthier ways. Let's make an example: John and Terry have been friends for years, since they were little kids. They may have had some quarrels now and then, but they usually make peace and go on with their lives, not putting too much thought into those instances. They have always had this tradition of making each other their favorite sandwiches for each other's birthdays. Nothing that require too much effort, but it always makes them smile, as it is their own tradition. Their birthdays are coming up, but John seems distant, Terry doesn't understand what's going on with him but think that it's best not to bother him. Terry thinks that a different sandwich, an upgraded version of the usual one he prepares for John, might make him feel better and cheer him up, maybe even make him laugh. The day comes, and when John unwraps his sandwich has a disappointed, almost angry look on his face. He looks at Terry, turns his back to the friend and goes straight home without letting Terry explain the situation. See, John thinks that Terry doesn't care about him, this is because Terry didn't ask John what was wrong in the last few days and he really wanted to talk about it but didn't know how to approach the topic himself. He has some trouble at home, and he is really upset about it, he needed stability and thought that Terry didn't even care enough to remember his favorite sandwich. This made him so sad that he decided to stay away from his friend for some time.

And there you go, friendship almost ruined just because of a miscommunication.

Everything could have easily been resolved if John and Terry had a sit-down and communicated everything that was happening and the reasonings behind their actions: Terry thought that John needed some space, whilst John wanted the company of his friend but didn't really know how to say it.

This is why understanding how to resolve conflicts is very important in one's life.

Exhibits of Conflict

Some say that conflicts are unavoidable and that can actually help you grow, and I can honestly agree with that, but I can also say the if you ask me, being able to resolve them thoughtfully can help you avoid many jarring and awkward situations as well.

Remember that your peers are living the same situations and issues that you do, maybe in a different form and maybe they act on them differently, but you all are on the same boat, so try and be understanding towards others.

Some tweens might have trouble with insecurities and anger management. This again is completely normal and understandable, but there are some boundaries you must respect in order to protect yourself and others.

Bullying isn't a conflict. Bullying is lashing out at other people for your own personal gain. This is a very toxic way to deal (or not deal) with one's emotions and it can lead to tragic outcomes. Bullying can take the forms of verbal abuse, physical abuse, cyber abuse. It is never ok and when it happens, actions must take place in order to avoid it or stop it in its tracks. Sometimes bullies come from dysfunctional homes, sometimes not. Either way, nothing justifies treating other people badly in order to make yourself feel like you have more control, more power. The power we are talking about it's not even real, because no one respects bullies, at least not for the right reasons.

Let's make an example to understand better what happens when someone is bullying someone else: let's bring back John and Terry. John likes rock music, whilst Terry likes classical music. These genres are very different, of course they are both music genres, but they usually have different audiences and different idols. John and Terry are discussing music, and Terry makes a point in why classical music is his favorite. John replies by saying why rock music is the best music. Terry feels a bit offended by John's statement, but John continues and says that while rock music is the best, classical music is the worst. Now Terry is very hurt by the words of his friend, and starts to think that listening to classical music is for lame people.

Now, of course classical music isn't for lame people, and preferences are only preferences, so why is Terry hurt by the words of John and why are John's words toxic? Saying that what you like is the best, isn't that bad, what's bad is trying to bring down someone else or someone else's interests in order to uplift yourself or your own preferences. The world is beautiful because everyone is different: if everyone was into rock music and only rock music it would be kind of dull and boring, wouldn't you say?

This is what happens with bullying. If you see someone being bullied or experience bullying firsthand, please communicate this with as many adults as you can.

Respect is the key word here, not only in the aforementioned situation, but with conflicts as well. You don't just need to respect the other person, but also, and most importantly, yourself: stand up for yourself, defend yourself and your views. Don't be afraid to speak your mind, but don't disrespect others while doing so.

Maybe your friends organized an outing and you were left out. This hurts and I get it, however this must not be an excuse for you to feel like you are justified to act out on your more than justified negative feelings. Don't lose control. You got this. Take a deep breath and step away from the possible conflict.

At-home-conflicts are also common, maybe a family member told you to do something you didn't want to do for whatever reason, and then you argued about it, maybe someone stole your favorite shirt to wear and you want to do something about it.

There are many instances in your life when there could be signs of incoming conflicts, but there are also many ways for them to be prevented or resolved in a mature, calm and positive manner.

How to Avoid and/or Resolve Conflict

In order to understand how to act when these situations take place, you need to know the different stages of conflict.

1. **Reasons why** ⇨ Conflicts don't happen without actual clashes. What does this tell us? It tells us that we have to

acknowledge how **everyone is and has to be entitled to their own opinion**. This doesn't necessarily have to cause conflict, but having different views on the same topics is a common human experience and it is the base of discussions, open dialogues and, from time to time, conflict.

2. **Clashes happen** ⇨ This step is the most obvious one, but it can sometimes be avoided. Sometimes other opinions may trigger us, may anger us: during those moments, lashing out and saying the first thing that comes to your mind and that could hurt the other person may feel like the most satisfying reaction you could have. However, this is the quickest way to start not only conflicts, but openly hostile conflicts, which are the worst. Remember to **always take a breath, count to 15 seconds and let it all go**. Answering fire with fire is never the solution, "kill them with kindness".

3. **Dialogue** ⇨ Whether it is hostile or not (again, hostility can be avoided), a dialogue or debate is going to happen. The goal here shouldn't be to win the debate, of course if that happens the better: your target is **not to prevail, but to be heard**. Your opinions matter, you shouldn't have to downplay other opinions in order to make yours look better, you can pinpoint the reasons why you think yours is better and cleverly debate the other opinions. None of these points NEED to be expressed through anger and hostility.

4. **Resolution** ⇨ This last point has to come, one way or another. Remember that **you have the power to fight for your ideas, as well as the tools to listen to others' opinions**. You have the right to admit when you are wrong,

the right of deciding if this is your hill to die on. You also have the right to step away from a toxic or hurtful situation, you have the power to do what you want, so do what you think it's right, but always remember that being kind goes a long way.

Empathy and Understanding Others

First of all: what is empathy? Empathy is the skill to understand, respect and possibly identify yourself in other people's feelings and emotions. Identifying yourself through someone else's feelings doesn't mean that you had to necessarily go through the same things that they have gone through or felt a similar pain: sometimes we empathize just by feeling sorry for them, or by understanding their triggers, their boundaries and their pain.

This is an example, and just for fun let's bring back John and Terry: these two best friends have a great friendship, right? You might say that they are the best of friends, even though sometimes they don't get along with each other, they always communicate and make peace. Maybe they have read our chapters on conflict resolution... Anyways, John and Terry go to the same school and attend the same courses. For one of these courses, they have to work on a project in pairs, so of course they decided to do it together. During the week that they had previously decided to dedicate to this project, John has a small bike accident and has to go to the dentist. It's nothing serious, but he has to take painkillers and is a bit shaken up by the scare. Terry has never had a bike accident and has never had teeth problems, so he can't really relate to John's problems, but feels very sorry for his friend. He decides to take full responsibility for the project for as long as the friend needs him to, even though nobody asked him to, and spends the next days working solo and texting his friend to keep him company and distract him. John is very grateful and feels less alone. He feels like he has a great and understanding friend. Terry knows that John would have done the same if the roles were swapped.

What could have been a source of resentment and sadness, strengthened their friendship instead.

This is the perfect example of empathy, a level of compassion and understanding we all have to strive for. It's not necessarily limited to friends, it can also be applied to family members or even strangers.

How to Show Empathy Towards Others

Now that the term "empathy" has been examined and understood: how do we apply it? There are some people that are born with strong empathy right from the get go, this can be a double-edged sword, because sometimes feeling other people's emotions too strongly causes them to ache and to be taken advantage of, because they are perceived as "too soft". Empathy isn't a disadvantage though, it is a great tool and the more we know how to use it, the more we will understand and respect others.

- First, we need to **examine other people's faces** when we are talking to them: do they seem happy? Upset? Sad? Angry? Not all people have strong facial expressions, but overall, this can be a great first step in learning what others may try to convey with their sentences.

- **Try not to be too impulsive with your reactions**: I know this can be hard sometimes, but it can bring you a lot **more self-control,** and the people around you may feel safer while expressing their feelings and emotions around you.

- **Listen** to what other people are telling you and try to focus on their actual words and how they are expressing them. Sometimes a shift in the tone can help redirect our behavior towards them.

- By trying to build empathy, **we become more self-aware** and consequently can create **stronger bonds** with our friends, family members and even teachers, so try and apply these tips to everyone you know. By understanding other people's struggles, you become more **open-minded** and accepting of others, which is always a great look.

- If you have problems understanding others, maybe you didn't understand the reaction of other people to your answers or what you were saying, maybe you think that a family member got angry with you without any good reasons, the solution is to **always ask questions**. Asking for clarification is always important and doesn't make you look stupid or ignorant. We have to learn from somewhere, so why not be open about your doubts, about situations you didn't quite get or about your own emotions? Sometimes even us adults don't understand why we feel a certain way, and keeping everything to ourselves can be detrimental both for us and for the people around us.

- **Be kind to others**, even if you feel like they don't deserve it. As previously mentioned, kindness goes a long way, and while I understand that sometimes it seems too hard, that it would make you feel better to just lash out, try and focus on the aftermath of our decisions. I remember when I was a tween and sometimes, I got angry at a family member and said some very harsh things. At that time, I only wanted to express how angry I was, I was even a bit vindictive at times. My anger got the best of me and I couldn't think of any other way to solve the situation, to make myself feel better and possibly hurt others in the process, or at least make them feel guilty. Let me tell you, not once did this behavior help me. Not even once. I felt guilty and sad as soon as those words fell out of my mouth and if it wasn't then and there, it was after a few hours, maybe even a day. I still bring that guilt with me because even though I have forgiven myself, telling myself that I was still learning and I was still a kid (which is true, by the way), I acknowledge that I could have done better, I could have handled the situation and myself in a completely different way. I hope you can learn from my past mistakes and understand this point of view I am offering to you.

Positive Relationships

How do we recognize which are the positive relationships in our lives? How do we build new ones?

Here are some tips on how to recognize the positive relationships in your life. These pieces of advice can be applied to almost any type of relationship.

- **Respect** ⇨ Do you feel like this person respects you? Do YOU respect that person? Do you feel like you are on the same level when you are talking to each other? Respect is the foundation of every relationship, so it is crucial to recognize it. When someone doesn't show us respect, we may feel humiliated, we may feel like our opinions don't really matter, we might feel misunderstood. Basically, spending time with this person makes you feel like you are alone. This doesn't necessarily mean that the relationship has to be immediately cut off. Usually, there is always room for progress, so the best way to go at it would be to talk about it with the person. This could make you feel awkward and scared, but it's all about their reaction: if they straight up judge you and don't understand where you're coming from, then you know this isn't working and to keep your distance from that relationship. They might come around and try to do better, it's up to you to decide whether you want to trust them again or not. Remember that you must be your number one priority and if you feel uncomfortable with someone, you must think about your own feelings first. If you are the one in the relationship that doesn't respect the other person, take a step back and ask yourself why are you behaving that way. Try to talk to the other person, ask for forgiveness, but if the other person realizes that she feels better without you in their life, let them be. This could be a great learning experience of what not to do with other friends or family members.

- **Acceptance** ⇨ This works the same way as how respect works. The questions you may ask yourselves are almost identical. The outcome too. If you love someone, whether it is a friend, a family member or others, you love them unconditionally. This means that you love your brother, even if sometimes you don't agree and fight over silly things, you love your parental figure even if sometimes they are strict to you. Love is accepting each and every part of one other, you feel comfortable with them nonetheless. You aren't judgmental with the person you feel close to. In order to not be judgmental, you have to stop being critical of your own self.

- **Trust** ⇨ Trusting others can be scary sometimes. This shouldn't happen when you're around the right person. You can trust them with your deepest secrets, because you know that they wouldn't judge you, and that they will keep their mouth shut.

- **Communication** ⇨ You feel like you can say whatever you want to them. If there is a conflict, you feel like you are able to talk about it and resolve it, because you can be open about those things with each other.

Cultural Sensitivity

The definition of this term is quite easy to imagine: "cultural sensitivity" is the acknowledgment and respect for the fact that many cultures other than ours exist, flourish and thrive both in different parts of the world and in our own as well.

Knowing and learning about other countries is absolutely necessary in order to be a good citizen not only of your city and country, but also of the world. Being educated is a power that we must value as crucial in our life, not only now as a tween, but also as a teenager, and later as an adult.

Different cultures have different habits, traditional dishes, possibly different holidays...it is incredibly beautiful, how varied the world is. We must be grateful for this diversity, as accepting and learning of its existence and diving into it will most definitely open your mind up to so much new information! You will be able to look at your peers that have different cultures than yours with respectful interest, you will be able to try different foods and learn how people in the West part of the world shake their hands when they meet while in Asia this is not the case and could actually be perceived as offensive. Kissing cheeks (even two or three times) when meeting someone could be very weird in America, but it's completely normal in the south of Europe.

If you want to be respectful to someone you just met that you know comes from a different culture, if you are going to visit a foreign country: do some research beforehand and ALWAYS be respectful of their ways. Some may look weird, funny or scary to you, but that's just because those things are new to you. Imagine someone that comes from the opposite part of the world that looks at your habits and laughs at them or is weirded out. You would feel a bit offended, right? You would like for them to respect your traditions and maybe even come to appreciate them. Well, there you go: that's exactly how they feel about this too.

If you want respect, you have to give respect, to be appreciated for your own culture you have to acknowledge and appreciate other cultures as well.

Chapter 3: Self-Esteem and Self-awareness

There are many reasons as to why developing your self-esteem and becoming more self-aware are very important steps to your growth, but we are going to narrow this down to two: for yourself and for others.

Let's welcome back our favorite best friends, John and Terry. This time let's bring another person in the mix. This other person is called Lucas, and he is a very energetic boy that tends to be a bit of a troublemaker. Lucas invites our two friends to go and do stuff they could get in trouble for. J&T aren't very sold on the idea, since neither of them likes to get in trouble and they don't really like Lucas, because of how rude he can sometimes be. They go anyway, because he is their friend and they don't want to disappoint him. When they meet up, Lucas is with some of his other friends, who immediately start mocking J&T. They feel small and weirded out by this situation. They start going around with this group but leave almost immediately. They later feel awful about themselves and promise not to hang out with those guys again.

John and Terry both committed mistakes in this experience: they didn't value themselves enough for picking themselves over the situation, and for this reason they felt the pressure of going against their wishes. They didn't have enough self-esteem to be prideful and walk away from something that didn't look like they would enjoy.

Lastly, they weren't self-aware enough: their behavior didn't match their own personal values, and this made them feel unbalanced and at high levels of discomfort.

In this chapter we will dive into these topics and we will learn how to use them for our own good and for the betterment of ourselves. By learning to have a good self-esteem and self-awareness you will also be able to build healthier and more honest relationships with the people around you.

Identifying and Managing Emotions

The first thing to notice is the facial expressions that you or someone else could pull whilst experiencing emotions.

There are seven universal facial expressions used to convey emotions and that have been recognized:

- Happiness
- Surprise
- Contempt
- Sadness
- Fear
- Disgust
- Anger

Remember that these aren't the only emotions that someone could feel, emotions are very complicated and not only there are a lot of them, but they can also be mixed: someone could both feel angry and sad, sad and happy, happy and surprised and so on.

To be more aware of your emotions, these are a few tips you can follow:

- **Recognize them** ⇨ Let's say that you realize that you are feeling a certain emotion, whether it is a negative one or a positive one. For this example, let's use happiness. Once you feel it, try and **track it**. Try and recognize when you feel it and why. Is it because you are eating a specific food you really like? Is it because you're in the company of a certain person? Is it because you did well on a test? By understanding when this emotion happens and which are the causes, you can either **seek them again or avoid them** (if you are tracking a negative emotion).

- **Give them a title** ⇨ By recognizing that you are experiencing an emotion and **naming it, you will be able to put a label on it and easily recognize it when you need to**. Also, it could be easier for you to talk about it and describe it if you are trying to tell someone how you feel or how a certain situation makes you feel. One emotion can have many different names, so do a little research or ask someone to teach them to you. The term that is used in order to refer to a specific emotion can indicate the level of that feeling. For example, happiness can also be described as "joy", "bliss", "contentment", "cheerfulness", "exhilaration" and so on.

- **Notice them in others** ⇨ in order to correctly identify emotions, you can observe others and try to understand what emotions they are going through. This can be done in two different ways: **by perceiving them through art**

forms and by watching the people around you. For the first one, the only thing you need to do is to listen to songs, watch movies or look at paintings. There are many different art forms and most of them were created through emotions. So not only a movie could make you feel something for the story or for the people portrayed in them, but you can also understand their own emotions. If a person in a movie feels vindictive, you could perceive their hatred, envy, jealousy, rage. You can also either empathize with the character, feel for them, be scared of what they could do. Same thing with songs and paintings. Some songs were made to express anger or sadness, happiness or love and so many other complicated emotions. Same goes with artists that paint. Van Gogh's work is riddled with his emotions and whether you like paintings or not, the pain and distress he went through while painting is undeniable.

- **Journaling** ⇨ This is not for everyone, so I get it if you don't want to do it, but let me tell you the benefits of journaling: a journal is a completely safe space that you and you only are allowed to enter. It's **your own bubble** where you can write down literally anything you want, whether you want to write down what happened during the day or express your concerns about stuff, if you want to talk about someone you have a crush on and you want to tell someone but you can't, you can write down your secrets, your anger... every little thing you want. It can be a great way to let everything out and, most importantly, to have a clearer view of everything. Sometimes we don't know how to express our emotions, sometimes we have anxiety and paranoia about stuff, writing it down puts it in

a whole other way, and we are more capable of understanding and dealing with it.

What to Do When Everything Feels Like It's Too Much

Regulating our emotions can be very hard. As I already mentioned before, when I was a tween, I wasn't very good at dealing with my own emotions. Since I didn't have people I felt safe talking to about these specific things, I was always lashing out and doing things I wasn't supposed to, then going home and getting very angry about everything. Now, in retrospect, I know I was only a tween with no sense of direction, completely lost in what was happening to my brain and body. I now know that if I had the set of skills to understand what was happening to me, I would have acted in a much calmer way and I would have most definitely understood others better. I only saw other people in correlation to me, not as their own person. My family members and friends all had lives that didn't concentrate around me. I know it seems obvious, but it can be a hard thing to remember whilst we are, for example, very angry at someone.

Sometimes we feel very overwhelmed and aren't able to understand why and how to calm down.

The tips we talked about in the last chapter can absolutely be applied to regulate our emotions, these are some more:

- **Triggers** ⇨ Since we are now learning to recognize and identify emotions, we can also understand what triggers them. Remember how we learned about asking ourselves questions about how and when do we feel certain emotions? Well, now we can apply this skill to **recognize**

when we need to step away from a certain situation. For example, you now know which situations trigger your anger, so whenever you find yourself in the same situation, you can act on it by stepping away, and if you can't, try and ground yourself. Breathe, distance yourself emotionally, keep your calm, be the bigger person.

- **Listen to your body** ⇨ Sometimes our body knows that an emotion is going to happen before your own brain understands what is going on. So, the logical thing to do is to listen to what your body tells you.

- **Be sincere with yourself** ⇨ Sometimes we don't want to feel a certain emotion, whether it is a good one or a bad one. This can be for many reasons, all of them understandable. What you need to do though, is ask yourself why you don't want to feel that emotion. Is it best for me to suppress it? What do I want to feel instead? Why? Lying to ourselves leads to not being self-aware, to not being able to talk openly about what we feel, to not understand ourselves. **Please, be sincere with yourself**, in your own brain. It is of the utmost importance to do so, and it makes everything so much clearer.

- **Talk to yourself in a positive manner** ⇨ Never tell yourself "I'm dumb", "I'm ugly" or anything that could bring you down, not even if it is a joke. Your brain picks up on what you say and can't really tell if it's a joke or not. It's the same dynamic that occurs when you are sleepy but aren't able to actually fall asleep. In order to help your body to doze off, you start breathing very slowly and relaxing each and every part of your body. At that point, your brain will say "oh well, I guess it's really time to fall asleep". Same thing happens when we talk poorly about ourselves. Your self-esteem will always suffer from this and you may surround yourself with a much more negative energy rather than a more positive one. Try being **your number one supporter** instead. Tell yourself that you got this, you are brave, smart and funny. You will see the difference it brings you.

- **Use your senses** ⇨ A trick you could use to calm yourself in stressful situations is to use your senses: sight (look at your surroundings, try and make a list of what you can see), sound (enhance your sound skills and search for every sound you can hear in this moment, even small ones), smell (same goes for smell, how many smells, odors and perfumes can you recognize?), touch (how many things can you touch? What are the textures you can imagine or recognize?), taste (if you are not eating at this moment, try and recognize the taste you have in your mouth, recall what your favorite and most comforting food taste like)

- **Talk to someone** ⇨ If you find yourself in a tough spot and you feel like everything is a bit too much, please seek the help of a professional. **Talk to the adults in your life** and express how you feel and what would you like to do about it.

Self-Awareness
What is self-awareness?

Self-awareness is the ability to align your actions to your inner morality. Everyone has their own set of morals and "internal laws" that we decide to go with or against. By being self-aware, you are able to be your most authentic self, and your mental health will benefit. This is one of the many reasons why you need to be the sincerest you can with yourself. Do you remember the example we made at the beginning of this chapter? The one about John, Terry and Lucas? By following Lucas and deciding to go with him, doing something they didn't really want to and later feeling guilty about their actions, they went against their better judgment. They didn't follow their morals and what they were comfortable with: instead, they went against their beliefs, just because they felt the social pressure of doing so. They weren't self-aware.

There are basically two states of self-awareness: the first one is public and the second one is private. We talked extensively about the second one, so let's dive a bit into the first one. Public self-awareness relates deeply with how you are perceived by others. Let's say that you don't want to do something but everyone else wants to. Those same people are trying to push you to do it, even by mocking you if you decide against it, but you end up caving in and do that thing anyways. Will you be happy about it later? What do you think will the others think of you? Trust me when I say that what the other people think about you is neither important nor necessary for us. Most importantly, we can't control what others think about us. Maybe we do everything in our power to please others, to do what we think they would like for us to do, but after all, they might still not like us. What does this tell us? It tells us that forcing ourselves to go above our boundaries in order to be liked by someone that doesn't appreciate you or your efforts, is only a waste of time. If someone is set on not liking you for any reason, that's their priority, but you don't have to deal with it. It is not your job to do so. Your only job is to be happy, and to be happy you have also to be self-aware. We can't control what others think of us, what we can control is how we deal and react to others, so why not focus on that?

Body and Mental Health

You don't have to be perfect. Say it out loud, say it in front of a mirror, say it to yourself as much as possible. Nobody is perfect, not even that one person that you think it is. No one, because everyone has their own flaws and struggles that they have to deal with.

As I already said in the previous chapters, asking for help isn't in any way a sign of weakness, it is actually a sign of self-awareness and sincerity and it is something that has to be welcomed with open arms. What if your friend came to you and admitted to you that they were struggling? You wouldn't judge them, right? So, why do we judge ourselves? We are human too, we can be flawed too, we can make mistakes too.

We can also take care of our body and our mental health, even before you perceive them as something that has to be dealt with. That means that you don't have to wait for something negative in your mental or physical health to come up to start prioritizing it.

Remember that having a healthy relationship with your body is more about how we feel in our own body and not our idea of what a body should look like. Erase the notion in your mind that a body has to look a certain way to be healthy or to look good. Every body is different, tweens like you are also still developing and growing. I understand that our society is really body-oriented, so focus on what "body positivity" is like and embrace yourself as how you are. You are perfect just the way you are and no one can change that. Remember, self-worth and self-awareness. You are your number one source of happiness for yourself, don't let the insecurities or meanness of others get in the way of your acceptance of yourself.

Don't compare yourself to others.

You are your own incredible person.

Mens Sana in Corpore Sano

"Mens sana in corpore sano" is a Latin phrase that basically means: "a healthy mind in a healthy body". Why the connection between body and mind? Because if your body is healthy, your mind is more likely to be healthy as well, and vice versa if your mind is healthy, it is more likely that your body is healthy too! Remember to do a lot of exercises if you can, and if you have the possibility, find a sport or two that you enjoy and pursue them. These sports must be ones that you not only enjoy and have fun doing, but that also make you feel happy and energetic. The repetitiveness is what's important, you have to be dedicated and keep practicing, be sure not to get stressed, otherwise it would become counter-productive.

These are some tips to stay healthy:

- **Keep eating healthy** ⇨ with the help of the adults in your life you can achieve a healthy diet full of the vitamins you need to grow. You can eat what you want, just be mindful and understand that sometimes we need healthier alternatives to grow better. Don't eat too much junk food, maybe save it for when you really crave it or dedicate a specific day of the week when you are able to eat whatever you want, but before deciding to plan this, discuss it with the grown-ups.

- **Practice sports regularly** ⇨ as previously mentioned, this is a great way to keep your body and mind healthy and to release some of the energy you have where it's right to do so!

- **Don't use your phone so much** ⇨ Now, I might sound like an old, grumpy guy that yells that technology is going to ruin us and all that. That's absolutely not what I mean. Phones and social media are a very big part of our lives, it's ok if we spend time using them, just not hours on end. Social media is mostly fake and advertising, it would be like watching the television and become indoctrinated by the shopping channel. Plus, mobile screens aren't very healthy to look at for too long, especially before sleeping. I'm not saying to cut it off, just to use it selectively and thoughtfully.

- **Spend time with your loved ones**, whether they are your friends or family.

Chapter 4: Decision-Making and Problem-Solving

Now that we have covered the major points of emotional control and we have acquired the set of skills needed in order to start understanding our feelings and the feelings of others, we can start learning how to manage them when needed.

In this chapter, we are going to learn about what "decision-making" and "problem-solving" are and how to achieve them in our day-to-day life.

In order to give you a rundown of the actual content of the chapter, here they are again, John and Terry to the rescue!

Do you remember that a few chapters ago I told you about the fact that our two best friends go to the same school and attend the same courses? Well, they do, and they really like to study together (mostly because they can tease each other and talk without being bothered by adults). At one of these study sessions, John opened up to Terry about a problem he was having with a specific subject. John told Terry that as much as he tried, he didn't understand it and didn't know how to approach this problem. Terry listens to his problems and tells John to wait for a couple of minutes, so that he could think about it. After some time has passed, he turns to John and starts talking. He begins by saying that he is sorry that John has been having these problems and asks why he didn't tell him before. John admits that he was too embarrassed to speak up about it. Terry assures him that there is nothing he has to be embarrassed about and that he understands him. He then asks John if he tried doing exercises and researches about the subject outside the assigned homework and John nods, but says that since he doesn't understand it, he wouldn't even know where to start researching and what to do with the exercises. Terry then asks John if he had thought of asking an adult in his house to help him with it, but John says that he tried and had been told from the adult that that subject wasn't something that they were able to help him with. Terry thinks some more, and then asks John if he had asked their teacher to help him. John tells him that that was what made him embarrassed. He thought that everyone in class looked like they had no problem and was afraid of being mocked or labeled as stupid if he was to ask the teacher for clarification. Terry then offers this solution: John will wait after the bell rings and their classmates are out of the class to ask the teacher to have a private chat, then he's going to tell the teacher about his doubts and worries and he's going to be honest about why he didn't ask for clarifications sooner. Terry offers to go with the friend, since John feels embarrassed to do it, and having his friend by his side could really help him to relax and feel safe.

John agrees, and later in the week they go to their teacher. John is able to speak honestly with the teacher who offers him to spend time together looking at the topics John is most confused about.

In this example, as we see, Terry has had the empathy to understand the discomfort the friend was having, and at the same time the critical thinking that was needed for an outside perspective. He studied the situation, asked for clarifications in order to have as wide a view as possible and then offered what he thought was the most logical solution to the problem, without forgetting about the emotional distress of his friend, and so adding himself as part of the solution.

Understanding the Decision-Making Process

For the purpose of acquiring the decision-making skill, we need to understand that in order to use it, we need to get access to the logical part of our brain.

Making thought-out decisions requires a good amount of patience and logic, so we need to tap into the part of our brain that uses logic and focus on that. In fact, in order to make better decisions, we really do need to avoid rash decisions and gut-feelings. There are many moments in which using our gut-feeling to make decisions is important and needed, but this is something that we are not going to be dealing with in these chapters, mostly because gut-feelings come from within you and are completely based on our instincts. This isn't something you can learn in a step-by-step process, it's just something we all have within ourselves, we just need to learn to hear them and feel them and, most importantly, when to listen to them. For example, if we are in a dangerous situation, our adrenaline has a big rush and guides us to safety before our brain can process what is going on. The gut-feeling we feel in those moments is basically our brain and adrenaline rapidly reacting to a situation and rushing to a solution. Maybe we are scared and feel like we don't know what to do, but underneath the fear and anxiety, the information we need is still in our brain, our gut-feeling is from us to us, telling us what we are too unfocused to understand. Does this make sense?

Well, in this chapter we are talking about normal decision making that doesn't involve adrenaline rushes and fear, so get comfortable, relax and let's dive in.

The Definition

Decision-making is the ability to choose something from a number of options and for that to be the best one for you, for other people or for both. It has a number of different factors, for example: the situation one's in, how others can be influenced by your decisions, what are the other options, your own state of mind you're in while making the decision, lots and lots and lots of questions you need to answer. Making decisions can be a difficult task for many different reasons, first of all being the fact that, in order to make the right choice and later be happy with what you choose, you have to think logically. Logical thinking is a priority while going through this system, and it works through a removal process: you will need to temporarily set the strong emotions that could affect your actions aside. Imagine that you need to make a decision regarding spending time with a person that has angered you. At that moment, you are just angry, maybe you feel betrayed and you don't want to analyze why you shouldn't feel that way .If you want to vent, that's ok: suppressing our emotions can be damaging and it's very unhealthy. What's not ok is acting on those negative emotions in an unhealthy way. If you were to spend time with said friend, you wouldn't be able to suppress your own anger, or worse: you would act on it and regret it later. Anger is a very complicated feeling and is to be managed with precaution. It can grow into various anger-ramifications, and it can lead to lots of outcomes. If not accepted and vented in a healthy way (sports, communication, listening to music...), anger can make us feel vindictive, unable to listen, prone to lashing out. What would happen if we decided to act on these feelings and made decisions based on those? I can 100% assure you that sooner or later, you will regret not having waited until you were in a calmer, more objective state of mind. In order to make decisions, you have to be able to be the judge, the practical observer of your own state of mind. Regarding the friend example, the best thing would be to decide between these two options: either you decide to spend time with them (but only if you are ready to calmly talk about the situation that angered you in a constructive manner) or it's best to let your friend know why you won't be seeing each other for the foreseeable future. If you need to calm down and stay away from a certain someone or a specific situation, it's best for everyone if you do.

You have to be able to listen to yourself and be ok with what comes up.

The Steps

First of all, you need to acknowledge the fact that you have to make the actual decision. You need to ground yourself and understand the situation as best as possible. Once you realize this, you need to know all the options you have and the different possible outcomes that choosing an option over another could bring you. For example, you want to eat some junk food, but it's close to dinner time. One option could be to eat the junk food and accept the consequences, whatever they would be. Your other option would be to avoid junk food this one time and decide on another specific time where you will be able to eat it, in a time which won't be as close to a prepared meal as this one. You need to evaluate each and every possible solution and option, all the outcomes and consequences. Essentially, you need to be able to gather all the information you can, so that you can make an informed decision. There is also the chance that the best thing for you to do is to not do anything, don't feel entrapped in a two-options-situation and remember that there is (almost) always a chance to get out (but not as a chance to escape making the actual decision)

Once you decide, you need to stick to your decision.

Remember to give yourself the time you need in order to be ready to decide. It's important that you choose without the influence of your own emotions or other people's emotions, but at the same time, take them into consideration. Will you or others get hurt by your decision? Will I be happy with the consequences?

Lastly, always remember that the world isn't black nor white, it's made from all the incredible colors of the world, all the different shades, all the nuances and undertones you could think of. Always take this into consideration.

Informed Decisions are the Best Decisions

What could be scary about making decisions? For instance, the responsibility of being the one making the actual decision, taking a stance, deciding for yourself or for others. Another thing that could be scary is not being able to access all the necessary information needed in order to start the process. You may be scared of being too emotional (too angry, too sad, too frustrated, too exhilarated) to make a decision and then later regret it. Most importantly, you could be scared of choosing the wrong option. Let's analyze every doubt and scary thought.

The Responsibility ⇨ You'll get used to it: **the more you grow, the more you have to decide for yourself** what's best for you and let me tell you, it is way better if you learn to do it from a young age, so that you will not be caught off-guard once you'll have more adult decisions to make. It's scary, but it is as scary as jumping from a cliff or a trampoline. The hardest part is the jump, but when the water hits you, you'll think: "was it really that hard to jump in the first place"?

Information ⇨ Just try and **put everything on paper**. Are there pros and cons? Time to write them down. Are there different plans to be created? Well, you guessed it, write them down. Try and imagine the different needed information as a percentage. In order to make the decision, you will need at least 90% of the probable information you can gather.

Emotions getting in the way ⇨ At this point you already know the drill: even if you think of being too emotional in the slightest, you need to **step away**, take a deep breath, distract yourself and **go back to the situation once you are calmer and more objective**.

What if I choose the wrong option? ⇨ I'm not going to lie to you: it happens. Sometimes we do all the right research, we take the right amount of time and make our pros and cons list and the result turns out to not be what we expected it to be. **It's ok, we can't be perfect and we can be wrong from time to time**. As long as you think you could have done everything you could do to make a thoughtful and informed decision, then there's nothing to be sad or angry about. Take this as a learned lesson and move on.

Generating Ideas and Creative Problem-Solving

Generating ideas isn't just a skill used to develop problem-solving abilities and managing to do it in a creative way: it also helps your mind to expand, it helps you to be more open about others' perspectives on many different subjects and it also helps to develop the ability to imagine situations and how to solve them.

This can give you the set of skills that you need in order to be a great problem-solver and to become more creative in the process, since creativity is incredibly important in your life.

Generating ideas can be hard, both for tweens and for adults too, so don't feel bad if you don't succeed at first, because it takes a lot of practice and patience.

This can also help you understand that failures and mistakes are a crucial part of your life. As already mentioned, nobody is perfect and you have to be loving and understanding with yourself. The expression "practice makes perfect" is true. Everything in life is practice. Of course, when you are passionate about something, everything becomes more natural and spending time by practicing your skills for something that you love doing doesn't feel like a task.

When I was 10 years old, I wanted to learn how to bike. I thought I was a bit too old to learn, but I discovered that there are some adults that never learned how to, so why would I be too old to start? The first time I tried to ride a bike it was a disaster, it seemed so easy when my friends were doing it, but as soon as I stepped on it, I lost my balance and fell. I came out of it with just a scratch, but I felt very embarrassed, so much so that I stopped trying and didn't want to even talk about bikes for months. But then I started thinking about bikes again and I told myself: "why not?". I fell again, but this time I didn't give up, and for many weeks all I did was bike around until I was so good at it that it looked like I was born for it.

It's not only perseverance, it's also patience.

The Definition

Problem-solving is the ability to analyze a problem in the most complete way possible. When one has this skill, one is able to look at a problem, identify the source of it, generate ideas in order to solve it, choose the best possible option and solve it. Lastly, we are able to look back and evaluate the solution and its outcomes, whether we made the right decision and what could have been done better, or how to never have to face that same problem ever again.

It is a great skill but again, it is almost completely logic-related, so we better put our thinking hats on and leave our emotions at the door, just for a little while. We need to be patient and understanding, empathetic but cool-headed, kind but firm. It seems hard, but as always, you have to practice (and sometimes fail) to learn and grow.

The set of skills required to be a good problem-solver are similar to the ones that are necessary in order to be a good leader, because they are focused on listening, respect and fast thinking.

Since each and every one of us, at one point in our lives, will need to be a problem-solver, why not try and make it fun? Being creative about it makes everything more interesting.

Firstly, we need to realize that everyone is creative, so this isn't even about being creative or not, it's more about asking: "in which area are you creative and how can we apply that to solving problems?".

Creating Creative Credible Solutions

In order to generate ideas, here are some steps you can follow.

Get ready ⇨ It's way harder to create ideas and think of solutions when you don't have any foundations. **It's best if you start from the root of the problem and work your way up**. Sometimes, this can be stressful and anxiety-inducing, so take one step at a time and start by focusing on the small things rather than the full picture right ahead. You'll notice that the full picture will become much clearer and easier to analyze once you are aware of every small little step.

Create ⇨ **Ideas will come**, sooner or later. You don't have to eagerly wait for them to just pop in your head, because they won't come if you go at it this way. It's like when you are waiting for a minute to pass: if you wait for 60 seconds and don't think about it, that minute will go by fast, but if you stare at the clock it will seem like more than a minute. Same thing with ideas, if you look for them at all times and ask yourself: "why don't ideas pop up in my brain?", they never will. It should be like gently placing a leaf or a stick at the spring site of a river and then rushing to its mouth to wait for it. Whilst waiting, you could find other leaves and sticks, both on the way to the end point and at the river's mouth, but you shouldn't think about the leaf while you wait for it, you should let your mind wander. At the end, your leaf will show up and you will go back home with more than what you went with. Remember that **opening your mind to different views it's always recommended and can lead to more creativity.**

Validate ⇨ Once you landed on an idea, **take some time** to sit on it. See how it feels and after you make it happen, evaluate it. This just means that you need to take a step back and try to look at what you've done in a productive manner.

If there is the need for a specific information from a person who feels uncomfortable sharing it, don't try to force them in any way, be understanding and try to figure out if you can help the situation without that information, because respect is always the key.

Why is Creative Problem-Solving so Important?

Practicing creative problem-solving leads to many different ramifications: you will be able to be more empathic, you could listen to others and better understand where they are coming from. You will learn that others may get affected by your decisions and how that makes you feel. You will learn, again, that not everything circles around you, and that other people have whole different lives that don't necessarily involve you completely. At the same time, you will learn to do your part in a relationship, meaning that relationships are never a one-way street, they go both ways and so, if you want a family member to be kind to you, you need to also be kind to them. If you want your friend to listen to your problems, you will need to be emotionally available to them. You have to show them that you care, that you are invested in their lives and their problems. Not only will you have to listen, but if needed, it would be best for you to also give them the advice they need. You need to love them and to not lie to them, because you don't lie to people you care about.

Problem-solving could also help you find new hobbies. See, sometimes in order to understand something we need to immerse ourselves in that thing. We can't solve problems if we don't know or understand the source, right? If we don't feel like solving specific problems is in our abilities, we have all the right to back down from the role of the problem-solver. However, if we really want to, if we have to, if we are interested in doing so, then there's nothing that can stop us. Remember what our first step is? Get ready, so if we want to be prepared, we have to know everything about the topic. Say you want to help a friend with a problem they have during an art class. If you want to truly help them, you need to understand the source, so whether you do some research, ask, or try firsthand, you will eventually get involved in the subject (the subject meaning an art class, or an art research of some kind, a research on a specific subject that the friend is struggling with...you get the gist). You could come out of the situation with a new interest, and if not, at least you have helped a friend.

Critical Thinking and Analysis

We are still in the realm of logical thinking. We have talked about how to make decisions, how to generate ideas, what is problem-solving and how to become a creative problem-solver.

Let's now look at the last topic of this chapter, which kind of embodies all of the other topics and at the same time, makes us better understand how to approach them: critical thinking.

In these last subchapters, you will learn how to work as cold-minded as possible. Did you notice that we went on a scale that started with us being logical and empathetic, then a bit more logical and rational to where we are now? So, what we are looking at right now is basically the top of this scale, from mixing rational and emotional, to learning how to think in the most rational, logical way.

This doesn't in any way mean that one way of thinking is lousier than the other, quite the opposite actually: what this teaches us is in fact that every little thing has a specific place and time to be in. Emotions aren't a part of critical thinking and should be understood and acknowledged but not used to make rush decisions. Being rational is good, but it also means to be empathetic and not cold-hearted towards others or towards ourselves. Lastly, empathizing with other people makes us better leaders, but only if we know how to compartmentalize.

Imagine your brain as a cabinet. Each drawer has a label on it which describes what's inside. Rational and critical thinking have been put in a drawer, emotions and feelings have been put in another. You can open them at the same time and mix up the contents, but you must know when, how and why you should or shouldn't.

The Definition

The term "critical" comes from the Greek word "kritikos", which means "having the ability to criticize, to judge". So, by this logic, critical thinking is basically the set of skills that makes you capable of perceiving something in the most complete way, logic-wise. If you are learning something and you aren't just absorbing information, but you are questioning it, analyzing it, looking at it from different perspectives and commenting on it, you are assimilating the information at its 100% value.

This is critical thinking, and no one is born with it. As everything we are talking about in this book, this set of skills is something you need to learn, and most importantly, you need to exercise quite often in order to improve on them and fully understand them.

An example: you want to make soup. A healthy yet tasty soup that everyone can enjoy. You can't just throw stuff in a pot and boil it, hoping that what comes out is edible. You first need to ask every person who would eat this soup, what ingredients they like and which one they don't like or can't eat for whatever reason. Then you make a list of what everyone can eat and what is to be avoided. On the side of the list that has what everyone would like, you have to analyze the ingredients and ask yourself what goes well with what, maybe by doing little experiments and taste tests. Once you have decided the final ingredients, you need to look up some soup recipes and see what would be best for you to follow, not only based on your ingredients, but also on your skills and abilities, on the time you have at hand to actually prepare it. You might also want to think of alternatives if the soup doesn't come out great. Then you need to buy those ingredients, even the ones for the other options, and you have to make sure that you are buying the right ones and the best ones (in terms of quality) that you can afford. After that, you need to start planning the actual cooking part, but before it, you need to know how long it takes to cook *that* or boil *those* or cut the vegetables and so on, so you can be as organized as possible.

And all of this is just for preparation. Do you get what I mean?

Some Advice to Improve Your Critical Thinking

Critical Thinking can easily be summarized in 5 steps:

Investigation ⇨ **Observing your surroundings**, what you know and what you don't know, **compiling lists** (it helps if you write things down, but it's not necessary) of things you need to know, pieces of information you have to gather, people you need to ask questions to... almost like a detective! This part is crucial, since without information we can't move forward, we can't understand what is going on and we definitely can't begin our critical thinking process. In fact, this is where the process actually begins. This is the foundation of our work, do you remember what we said about building a house, right at the beginning of the book? We said that there is no house without foundations. In this case, our foundation comes from investigating and information gathering. Once you think you have enough of those, you can move on to the next step.

Analysis ⇨ Ok, so now we have all the information we were able to gather. Imagine that they are right up on a wall, just like a detective would put them. You are the detective in this scenario, right? Try imagining yourself in this room, with one of the walls all covered in sheets of information, plastered with facts and details. What would a detective do? They would sit down in their chair in front of that wall and **analyze every single thing there is** on there. They would realize that there are connections from one piece of information to the other, they would take a piece of string and piece all those details together. Link them in a way that they wouldn't have been able to if there wasn't a literal wall of information right in front of them. That's analyzing: piecing together the information, making links, studying them.

Deduction ⇨ What the detective does next is solving the crime, right? What does that mean for us? This means that it's time to make those connections make sense. To find the solution to the conundrum or, to put it simply, to **completely and fully understand the information**.

Decision-Making/Problem-Solving ⇨ This is where everything connects. We talked about all of these topics in depth and we now know that, if there is the need, you will be able to apply critical thinking in order to solve problems.

What Would I Need Critical Thinking For?

Critical thinking is crucial for more things than you would think. It's essential for studying, especially the subject where logical thinking is needed the most, like science, math, grammar and so on.

By learning and mastering critical thinking, you will be able to make connections not only in the subject themselves, but also between different ones. This will help you study better and faster. I know that what we described until now, all those needed steps, seem long and difficult, but by exercising them and following them as much as possible and as often as possible, things will become easier and easier.

You will also better understand which are your weakest and strongest skills. You will be able to look at them and strengthen them or use them at your advantage. That's because critical thinking will make you capable of watching yourself from within, you will understand yourself better, analyze your mistakes and learn from them.

That goes for your social life too! Not only will you be able to understand which of your friends are the true ones, but you will also be able to be the best friend you could be, because you will become more understanding and empathetic, you will form stronger bonds and be an active listener. You will notice how people will feel more comfortable with you, more open and sympathetic. Not only will you be able to listen, but you will be listened to.

That being said, there's one thing I really want to tell you: don't be hard on yourself. If you make mistakes at school, with your friends, with family members... It's alright. It happens. It doesn't imply or mean anything other than the fact that people aren't perfect. It's not the mistake that's important: it is how you react to it that matters. Being sad, angry or hurt is normal and understandable. You will need to process those emotions and later understand what you can do about the situation, how to go about fixing those mistakes. Remember that communication and honesty are always crucial.

Chapter 5: Practical Skills for Daily Life

In this chapter we will talk about independence. Whatever your family and house situation is, learning to do some stuff for yourself is always helpful, both for right now and for later in life. As always, if you learn to do stuff now, you won't be lost in the future.

This episode of John and Terry is going to be just about this.

John and Terry have many friends, we met one of them a few chapters ago and his name is Lucas. Let's introduce a new friend: Max. Max is a happy, easy-going person who loves sports and has a passion for movies. John and Terry have met Max in class, and they have been friends ever since. Sometimes, the three of them go on little adventures together and they always have fun. One time, during recess, they came up with an idea: they all liked the same movie and they were talking about it. They were remembering a scene in the movie where they prepared something to eat, and they thought it looked delicious. Max widened her eyes and exclaimed: "I've got it! What if we do a movie party, just the three of us. We watch this movie together but before that, we prepare that delicious dish they eat in it, so that when they eat it, we do as well!". They all cheered and thought it was an amazing idea. They all individually asked the adults in their family if they could do it, and they all got the green flag, but only if they had one of the adults to supervise them at all times. They were ok with that and so, they began planning. The adult would accompany them where they wanted to go and would help them in the kitchen when needed, but other than that, they would do everything by themselves. They planned by calculating the hours they needed to go get groceries and go back, how long would it take for them to cook the actual meal and how long the movie is. After that, they looked at all the ingredients they needed and calculated how much each of them had to spend for the shared meal. They decided to split things evenly. They then asked for the adult family member to accompany them to the market, then later they prepped the ingredients and started the cooking process, but left the dangerous parts to the adult (as previously agreed upon). After that, they were able to enjoy the movie while eating the meal they all prepared together, all the while having a fun afternoon doing everything together. They later cleaned up after themselves, and decided to make that a recurring event.

Time-Planning and Management

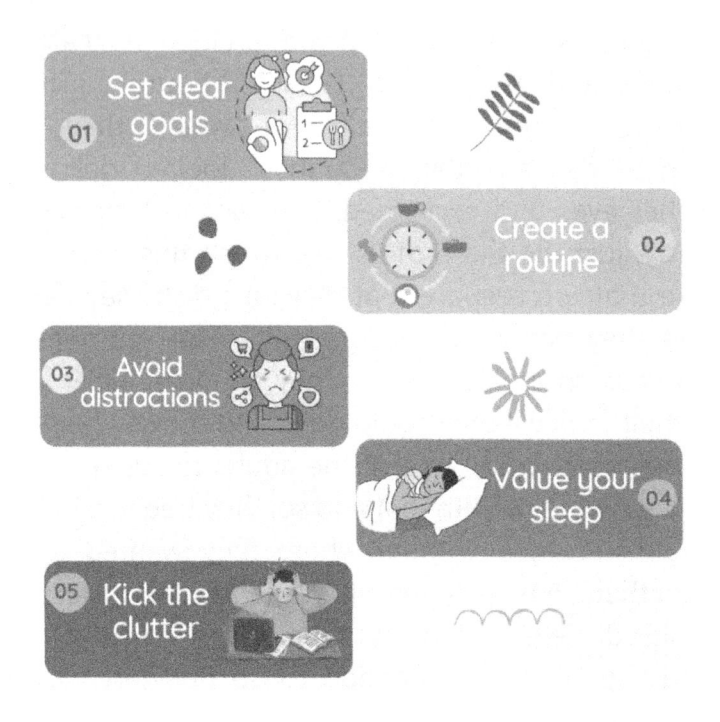

01 Set clear goals

02 Create a routine

03 Avoid distractions

04 Value your sleep

05 Kick the clutter

What is time-management? Time-management is a very important skill you should practice whenever you have a chance to.

As a tween, you will probably experience a surge of tasks, responsibilities and homework: you will have to study more. Your own personal time is going to be affected by this situation, one way or another.

Suddenly you will feel like the time you had to play or just simply for yourself, isn't the same as before. Maybe you will be asked to be more helpful around the house or to spend more time studying whilst at home.

This is why planning your days ahead could be very important.

Remember that the more you grow up, the more things will change: I know this can sound scary, but trust me, you have everything under control.

By being able to manage your time, not only will you be able to do things in a quicker way, but you will also be able to have even more free time on your hands!

In the next three chapters you will be able to understand how time-management works, you will learn what it takes to have this skill, how to work for it and how to master it. You will learn where and how you should apply it in your day-to-day life and, most importantly, why should you.

As always, it could seem like it's overwhelming or hard, but trust me when I say that applying these things in your daily life is way easier than it sounds.

It's like this: imagine that you are an expert in building cabinets, you have been doing it since you were little and could do it blindfolded (but you shouldn't because it would be dangerous).

You now have to instruct someone else on how to build one, but here's the catch: the other person doesn't have the slightest idea on where to start. They know the basics and could think of a few ways they could do it, but don't really know where to even begin the process. As someone that is an expert on the topic, you start describing the process. It seems easy for you, because you have done it so many times, but your friend asks you to slow down and tell him what to do step-by-step. You do it, and once they truly understand what they are supposed to do, they tell you: "this is way easier than what you were telling me!". This seems unnerving, but it is understandable: having to physically do the job makes the instructions have more sense. Same thing applies here.

Why Should You Learn to Manage Your Time

As already discussed, time management can be crucial to not get stressed out, to not get too overwhelmed with the amount of tasks you may have to accomplish throughout the day, but it would also help you as a stress relief method, it could help you to be less anxious about how many things you have to do and how much time you have on your hands to do those things.

Imagine that you have to study for some tests at school, but you also have to do some chores around the house and at the same time you have to tend to a pet, but you also have to do a physical job (e.g., mowing the lawn or babysitting) for an adult family member that promised you some money if you did what they asked you to. It seems like a lot, almost too much. Most people, when approached with this amount of tasks, have two different approaches: the first one would be to eliminate one or two of the tasks. Maybe the money-earning one, maybe the study session. The second approach would be to do everything as fast as possible in order to be able to end the day with everything done, but at the same time being incredibly stressed and tired.

I'm not saying that these approaches are wrong, what I'm saying is that a third method exists, and it is to plan ahead. Manage your time properly, look at all the tasks you have to complete, put them each in a specific time frame and try to, if possible, add time-outs in between in order to take the stress off however you want to.

Some days are just like this: too full, too stressful, but if they happen, we should make sure to take the next day off, at least of some of the chores and tasks you should do. Time management is also for situations like this.

What's important to remember is that no matter how many things you have to do, no matter how many responsibilities you may have, your mental health is the number one priority.

Sure, planning ahead and time management help you to organize your days, hours and minute in order to be able to get more work done and to do it in the best way possible, but the real goal here is to alleviate the stress, to make sure that your mental and physical health is strong, that you are happy.

Tips for Time-Planning

Here are some tips on how to advance your skills in time management. These can be all applied to almost any situation. Whether you have to plan your day ahead, a specific event, a study session or more, these are the tips for you.

- **Identify the goals** ⇨ This first step is crucial: you have to obtain a **clear view of the situation** and of **what you want to achieve**. For example, you want to be able to do everything you need to do but still have time to relax and pursue a hobby. This free time should be your goal. You want to receive a good grade at school, and for this reason you have to plan a few study sessions? Your goal is a good grade, and you should focus your planning around and towards that.

- **Create a timetable** ⇨ This is something you can do anyway you want, even with a sheet of paper that you can hang in your room. In this timetable, you can **write down the hours of the day and what you have to** (or should) **do** during those selected hours.

- **No distractions allowed** ⇨ This might feel a little self-explanatory, but hear me out. Do you remember when we talked about how to study? The same tips can be applied here as well. The only difference is that the "no distractions allowed" we talked about there is more generalized here. Once you have done an hourly plan, you will be able to follow it, but only if you **keep your focus**. Let's say that you have to go to school, go back home, do some house chores and have some time for yourself. If you decide to spend some time with your friends right after school, you can (if you inform an adult family member and they are ok with it), but you need to understand that by choosing that, you won't have the relaxing time by yourself later.

- **Prioritize** ⇨ Let's say that your main goal is to study. Sometimes we don't really want to do what we have to, but we must, so if there's something you must do, that instantly becomes your number one priority. **Your timetable should focus on that and then build the rest of the hours of the day around that**.

- **Be kind** ⇨ Take some time off between each task and **don't be too hard on yourself**.

Some Tools for Time-Management

There are many tools that we can rely on and that can help us with time-management. Some of these can be found online, or can be downloaded, so ask for the help of an adult to download them or just to make sure that they are safe to be applied to your routine.

- **Time Managing Apps** ⇨ There are some specific apps you can download on your devices (phone, tablet or computer) that were specifically created with the goal of helping people with digital lists, reminders you can, set and so on. If you want to go down this route, please seek the help of the adult family member.

- **Time Planner** ⇨ As already mentioned in the previous post, a timetable or time planner is the number one tool you can have. It is the most complete, since it has everything you need in order to be organized and to plan in and of itself. Time planners usually have an incorporated master list.

- **Lists** ⇨ Just like the master list we just mentioned and the ones that should be made before grocery shopping, a "to-do list" is just what it sounds like: a list of all things you can think of that have to be done or completed. It can be developed at the beginning of a month, a week, a day or even just the few hours that are ahead of you. The more lists you can make, the more you will be able to have under control.

- Set a **timer**

- **Complete the most dreadful tasks before everything else**

- Purchase a **calendar**

Budgeting and Money-Management

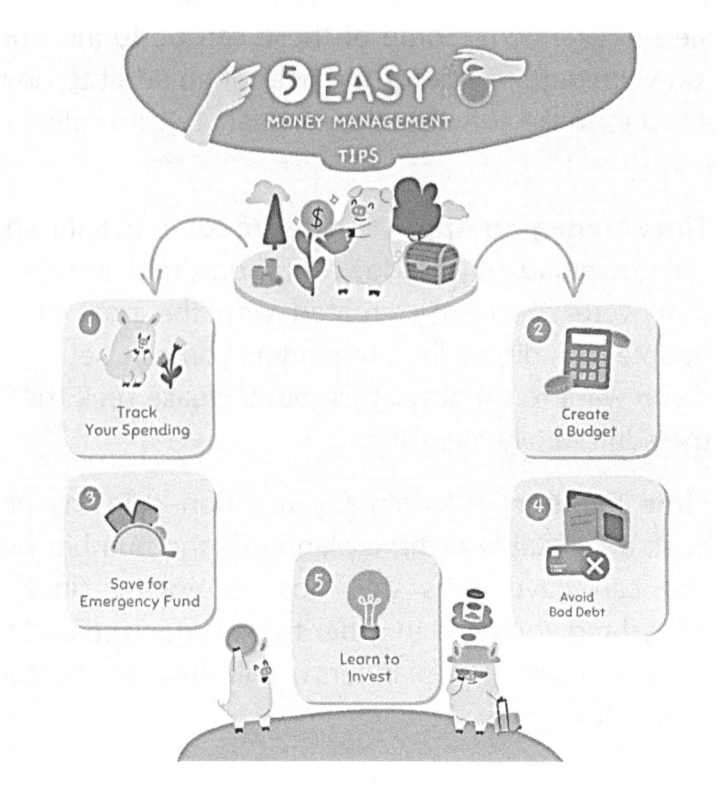

5 EASY MONEY MANAGEMENT TIPS

1. Track Your Spending
2. Create a Budget
3. Save for Emergency Fund
4. Avoid Bad Debt
5. Learn to Invest

As a tween, there are some things that are going to change: you are starting to grow, you are officially leaving childhood behind, but you aren't a full-blown teenager yet. Your brain is quickly developing and you are learning more and more things. This is usually the time in your life where you are able to retain the most information. Picture yourself as a sponge that soaks up as much water as it can.

This is the reason why money-management is better to be taught now rather than later. The best time to learn how to handle money and how to budget is during these years, because, as we already mentioned, you should learn this stuff sooner rather than later. If you know how to handle money now, you won't be lost in the future. You will remember what you are learning right now and you will know what to do right then and there.

During adulthood, budgeting and managing-money is incredibly important. It is a crucial part of our life, and it helps us get by easier.

Do you remember when John, Terry and Max had to plan their grocery trip ahead? What did they do? Firstly, they made a list about everything they had to buy for their delicious movie dish, and then they decided which alternative they needed if the dish turned out to be a flop. They then went on by adding up all the prices of each ingredient and deciding to split the total evenly, because it seemed like the logical thing to do, since they had about the same amount of money on hand and they would have all benefited from what they were purchasing.

After taking everything into consideration, they went with it.

All of them agreed on everything, which was and will always be extremely important.

What Do I Need to Know About Money-Management?

The most crucial thing you need to know is the difference between what we want and what we need.

Let's go back to grocery shopping: let's say that we have a certain amount of budget to use. You decide what to buy based on that budget. When you are at the supermarket, you see something else that wasn't on the list but that you really want to take. You decide to buy it, and then you learn about the consequences of your actions: since you took something just because you wanted it, and by doing that you didn't take into consideration the budget that was predetermined, you weren't able to buy everything that you needed. Well, at the beginning you don't feel too guilty about it, because at least you have the thing you really wanted, but soon after you'll recognize that the consequences are deeper than that: the things you weren't able to buy were important for the household. You ended up making a mistake just because you didn't think about the alternatives. For example, if you would have waited for the next trip to the grocery store and informed the adult family member of what you wished to buy beforehand, you would have been able to come out of the store with what you wanted AND with all the other stuff you went to buy in the first place, both things done while respecting the budget.

We have learned that the difference between "wanting" and "needing" is crucial in money management, since it can make us more aware of what's essential and what's not. Whether you already have your own money or not, respecting this ground rule is essential. You always have to budget your money, so that not only you know which and how much money you have for essentials, but also why and how much money you have left for your own interests.

Let's say that you have, or will have a part-time job and that you really want to buy something that costs a lot. What you need to do is budget your money and with patience and perseverance, you will be able to save enough to buy it.

The first time I was able to buy something with my own money it was something I really wanted for a very long time, but I had to save up for months and months. It seemed like forever, but the feeling of finally having what I wanted in my hands, and having it thanks to my hard work and patience... was priceless.

Tips for Budgeting

Here are some tips for money budgeting. Keep in mind that these are basic tips that will lay the foundation for your approach to money later in life.

As of right now, the best thing you could do is to ask for someone, for example, the adult family member in your house that you can rely on, to help you understand these tips better and who could give you some practical exercises for when you want to practice these pieces of advice:

- **Mistakes happen** ⇨ Don't be too hard on yourself when, whilst budgeting money, you make a decision that turns out to be wrong. **We all learn through our mistakes**, so don't judge yourself too harshly, learn to look at the mistake and see it as a valuable lesson of what you shouldn't do in the future.

- **Want vs. Needs** ⇨ We already talked about this: you are 100% allowed to wanting something, **it's just a matter of priority**! What you want corresponds to what you need? If not, plan ahead and make sure to save for the things that may not be necessities but that you would like to have.

- **Control** ⇨ "Control" is a powerful word that can be applied to this topic in two different ways: the first version of control we need is **the one we exercise on ourselves**. Let's say that you did everything right but, once faced with different options, you feel like you're pushing yourself towards the "wants" and not the "needs". I assure you that you will regret this in the long run, so try and remember the priorities and focus on looking at the big picture: if you allow yourself to be patient, you are not missing out on anything you want, on the contrary, by waiting you will be able to get everything. The other version of control that we can apply here is **something that solely relies on your budget**. By checking how much money you saved at the end of each month, you will be able to have more control over it.

- **Make lists** ⇨ In order to actually control what goes in and what comes out of your savings, you should **write down every single penny you used, and the purpose of that spending**: if you went out and bought something to eat, you make a note of it as soon as you go home, so that you don't forget about it. Make sure to describe all the specifics of what you bought, so that you can later come back to them if needed.

Some Tools for Money-Management

As for money-management, the tools that are available in order to help you and guide you in your money budgeting journey can be found both online and not, so always ask for the help and permission of the adult if you want to search for something like this on the internet.

- **Apps** · Exactly the same as time management, there are apps which were **specifically designed to help** you track what you earn, what you spend and what you put aside.

- **Online resources** · If you think that's what you need, then by all means look into it, but **always with the permission and supervision of an adult.**

- **Piggy bank** · Piggy banks don't always come in the shape of cute piggies (I know, what a disappointment), they actually come in all shapes and sizes, sometimes with a security system as well, for example, a lock or some keys. They might seem a bit childish, but let me tell you a little secret: I have one. I know, it seems silly that a grown-up has something like this in their house, but it's so incredibly useful! You see, I do have money in the bank, but I also have cash, both in my wallet and hidden away in my home. This is for **security** and for emergency purchases, so by having a piggy bank, I actually feel safer, since I know where my extra-money is and how much is it. I wholeheartedly recommend it.

- **Planners** · Lists and planners are so crucial for so many things. Remember that we are now talking about all the **things that require organization and precision**, and what better tool we have than books and sheets of paper we can write on? You can also use a computer program to make charts, so don't worry about it. Anyways, planners of any kind are essential for managing things, from time to money... to some other topics we're going to dive into later.

Cooking and Meal Preparation

There are times in our lives where we are at home and want to eat because we are hungry. The fast solution would be to eat some junk food that doesn't need any type of preparation, or to eat something that should be good once prepared, but either we don't know how to, or we are too lazy to cook. Maybe there's going to be some days where you will be in charge of prepping your lunch-box for school.

Well, these next chapters will guide you through the basics of cooking. You don't need to know how to prepare incredibly elaborate meals or how to bake sweets, just the basics will do for now, and if you want to learn more, you can always ask an adult to help you.

By the way, there are some things you should avoid doing, because they might be too dangerous to do by yourself. If you really want to do those, you should again ask an adult for help. They could support you through the different steps, or they could do it for you.

Some people really like cooking, others don't. Either way it's fine, you shouldn't force yourself into liking something you don't. However, some things are to be learned and mastered even if we don't like them.

What will happen when you will live by yourself in some years? Even if you have roommates, it won't be their job to feed you, so you should learn to be independent and manage yourself in a healthy, safe way.

Whilst cooking their delicious dish, John, Terry and Max didn't do everything themselves, remember? They asked for help from the adult that was supervising them, and while the adult was doing the things they weren't allowed or didn't feel safe doing on their own, they prepared what they knew they could on their own.

They knew when to leave stuff for the grown-ups to do, and they also knew which were the things they could do on their own, and they did them.

Always be aware of your surroundings and try to have fun while cooking.

Basic Cooking Skills and Techniques

This chapter will be divided in two sections: the first one is going to be about basic tips you need to learn and remember once you enter the kitchen; the second one is going to focus on the things you can start practicing. Always ask for the adult's permission beforehand.

- **Wash your hands** ⇨ This tip is absolutely crucial, both in general and in the kitchen. You should be like a surgeon, who cleans their hands thoroughly every time they have to do their job. You, as a little chef, need to remember this first rule religiously. You should **wash your hands before touching anything in the kitchen, but also during the process**. What if you're preparing a pizza: you are kneading the dough and after that you go straight to the kitchen utensils you need? You would dirty the utensils with sticky flour and oil, they would become unmanageable and they could slip away from your hand and you make a complete mess. So, ground rule: wash your hands.

- **Prepare the ingredients ahead** ⇨ This isn't a really strict rule, but it's something that could become pretty useful for a good reason, which is that by having everything already measured (you should learn how to measure ingredients) and set, you won't have to rush through everything in the search of one ingredient you forgot about, and don't immediately know where to find, or how much of it is needed. Sometimes **timing in the kitchen is essential**.

- **Learn the language** ⇨ There are some **specific terms** that are used in the kitchen and that you should learn, such as the **name of the utensils** (pans, spatulas, pots...), or the name of some basic **procedures**, like boiling, frying or roasting... don't worry, all of these can be learned along the way.

- **Follow the recipe or the instructions** ⇨ As a first-time chef, you don't need to improvise. Actually, you really shouldn't. You should know the rules in order to know how to bend them, right? So, if you don't know the rules yet, how could you improvise? Be careful, don't make rash decisions and **follow the step-by step recipes**.

- **There's no rush** ⇨ This isn't a cooking competition, there isn't a prize if you are the fastest. Incidents happen in the kitchen, make sure to be always supervised and **take your time** to do what you need to do. No one is chasing you.

These are some examples of stuff you could start doing in the kitchen. I know you are probably tired of hearing this, but remember to always have an adult with you that can guide you, help you, supervise you and handle the stuff you shouldn't do on your own.

- **Grating cheese or peeling vegetables and fruits**

- **Chopping vegetables** (this only applies if an adult allows you to, and if you are already learning how to handle a knife)

- **Prepare a sandwich**

- **Bake cookies or muffins**

- **Draining pasta** (watch out for the hot water!)

- **Making bread**
- **Cooking eggs**
- **Preparing the ingredients**
- **Whisking**
- **Preparing salads**

There are a lot of other things you can learn, just talk to the adults in your family if you want to learn.

How to Prep a Meal

If you have been practicing with your cooking skills and you got the green light from your family, you can go on to the next step, which as the title suggests, is meal-prepping!

Here's how you prepare a meal, in a step-by-step basic guide.

- **Decision-making** ⇨ Now it's time to apply all the skills you now have about decision-making. **You have to take into consideration all the facts**: are you the only one that is going to consume the meal? Does the meal need a time frame of preservation? Is it hard to make? Will I be able to prepare it, with the help of someone else?

- **Taste** ⇨ This is one thing you need to take into consideration, whether you are preparing the meal for yourself, for others or for both. If you aren't aware of other people's tastes, it's best to ask. This also includes allergies.

- **How healthy is it?** ⇨ The meal doesn't always have to be 100% healthy, but it would be best if it is, at least as much as possible. To fully understand what's healthy and what's *unhealthy*, why and how to mix those two, try and do your research, ask some adults if you want to be sure.

- **Make a list** ⇨ When you have finally decided what to prepare, you should **compile a list of all the ingredients you need**, whether you think you already have them in your home or not. Make sure to include everything you could think of: all the ingredients have to be listed, even the spices. If the recipe includes salt and oil, include them in the list. In addition, you should also include the things you may need to prepare it with: if something needs to be boiled, you should list that you may need a pot.

- **How much do I need?** ⇨ This is where the money management we talked about comes in handy. You should **divide the previous list between things that you already have at home and the things you have to buy**. Ask the adult family members for the information you need. Once you know which of the ingredients you need to buy, **ask for the prices of all the things** and if you don't know them, you could ask for an adult in your life to accompany you to the grocery store, make a list of how much does everything cost. At that point, you can go back with the right amount of money and purchase what you need.

- **Time-Management** ⇨ Make sure to **plan the meal ahead**. All recipes usually include the duration of the cooking process. Depending on how much time you have in order to do it, how much time you need to prepare for it, how long everything takes.

- **Gather the ingredients** ⇨ Bring to the kitchen the ingredients you purchased and the ingredients that were already home.

- **Set the ingredients**
- **Prepare the meal**
- **Serve it or put it away** ⇨ Make sure to use the right containers to put things away. Ask your adult family member **how to preserve** the meal.
- **Clean after yourself**

Safety first!

I know, I know, I already told you a million times, but your safety is the number one priority.

In order to be as safe as possible, the first thing you should do is try to be as objective as possible. When I was a kid, I was very adventurous, but there is a limit between adventurous and silly, right? What is the difference? "Being adventurous" means having the desire to experience new things and to push yourself to do new stuff, it's an amazing character trait! It becomes dangerous once you start being silly about it!

I'm going to tell you a story: when I was a kid, I was very active and energetic, I would get bored quite easily and I was quite adventurous, as I said before. One time, I was at home and I was incredibly bored. I had done my study for the day and I was home alone. My boredom turned into hunger (it happens sometimes) and I decided to make myself some eggs. Mind you, I had never done eggs before, but I figured, well, it can't be too hard, can it? Everything went miraculously well, that was until I had to turn on the stove and put the pan on it. I didn't think it through, and I burnt myself. It hurt and I was surprised, so I let go of the pan and uncooked egg went EVERYWHERE. The burn itself wasn't that bad, it went away with the right medication in just a few days, but I learned two pretty important lessons:

1.DON'T USE A PAN IF YOU DON'T KNOW HOW

2.The difference between being adventurous and being silly is arrogance. I was so pretentious that I didn't look at the situation, not really. My only thought was "pff, I can do it!", like I was in a competition with myself.

Please, be humble. When you look at a knife and you want to use it to chop the vegetables next to it, ask yourself: do I know how to use it? Could somebody help me? Do I know the rules one needs to know in order to use a knife?

There's no shame in asking for help.

Literally zero.

House Responsibilities

Listen, I know I already told you many cautionary tales about my pre adolescent years, but if there is one thing I was very good at, was to take care of my house, and this is the reason why.

Do you remember my incident with the eggs and the pan? And how I accidentally spread raw egg all over the kitchen? Well, the episode doesn't really end there. After the shock of what had just happened passed, I looked at my surroundings and I discovered the mess I made. My immediate reaction wasn't: "my parents are going to be so angry!", I decided to take things into my own hands. Firstly, I put my hand under some cold running water from the kitchen sink, because I knew that when you suffer from a burn, you need to immediately put it in contact with something cold. That made me sigh of relief. After that I started cleaning the kitchen. Wherever I saw the clues of raw eggs (and there were a lot), I cleaned. I later explained what happened and my parents were mostly worried about me and my own safety, and lectured me about what I was and wasn't allowed to do. As I said, a hard learned lesson, but still a good one that I bring with me to this day and that I passed on to my own children.

What I want you to understand, is that I didn't clean because someone told me to, I didn't do it because I was afraid of my parents' reaction: I did it because I respected (and still do) the people I lived with. I knew that the mess I made was of my own doing and so, it was my own duty to clean it up. If my parents or siblings made a mess, they didn't expect me to clean it, so why should I?

And it's not even because they are my family, it's because I lived with them and I respected them. I understood that my own room was my personal space and the rest of the house (except for the other bedrooms) was common space. If I wanted the common space to be clean, I had to do my part, which consisted in cleaning after myself, putting away my toys when I wasn't using them and doing house chores if I was asked to.

I admit I was a bit troublesome from time to time, but not because I didn't respect the people around me. I learned what respect was when I was way younger, and I still cherish the meaning of it as of now.

To respect and to be respected is important, and it starts in the household.

Cleaning after yourself and helping with the common spaces is a part of it.

How Can I Help? – Personal Space Edition

Well, the question "how can I help" is a great start in and of itself.

You shouldn't take anything for granted, especially with the fact that in some years you won't live with other people that will automatically vacuum your bedroom, clean your windows, or even fold your clothes and underwear. You will have to learn not only how to do all these chores yourself, but to also be aware of how much it can be done for a much more relaxed environment. If you already know how to though, good for you!

So, how can you actually help? For starters, let's analyze what we talked about in the previous chapter some more: personal space and common areas.

You could say that your own room is your personal space, but if you share your room with someone, that doesn't mean that it automatically becomes a common area, it's more like a shared space, but you still have personal space in there. Your bed and the space around it, for instance. One thing you should know how to do is to keep your own personal space clean and tidy.

Do you remember when we talked about how to study? Well, it's kind of the same thing: if you keep up with your study, you won't have loads of stuff to study with no time to do it right before an exam. Same thing applies here: if you keep your space tidied, you won't deal with a messy room and you won't be confused on where to even begin cleaning it up. I get it, sometimes life gets in the way and you're not always in the mood for cleaning, and that's absolutely understandable. If push comes to shove, don't panic. Start with the thing that seems the hardest, for example picking things off the floor and putting them where they are supposed to be, and then go on to the next thing. One thing at a time, and if needed, take breaks and go back to it when you're ready again.

The best scenario would be to be able to keep everything in its right place from the start. So, a good habit you can grow into is to, right after using something, putting it away. If you have a pile of clothes that are half-dirty, half-clean, use a chair or a closed space to keep them and, if possible, don't use other clothes until you finish using that pile.

Having a clean and tidy personal space isn't only nice to look at, but it has an incredibly good influence on your ability to focus and on your own mental health.

How Can I Help? – Common Area Edition

The basics on how to keep your personal space tidy are done, now let's move on to the common areas.

Some common areas that you can find in most homes are the kitchen, the living room, the hallway and sometimes the bathroom. Keeping these areas clean and tidy is a shared chore between all members of the family: that's not only because everyone uses them, but also because everyone's personal items are there. It can be a brush or some hygiene products in the bathroom or some books and toys in the living room. Everyone is entitled to their personal belongings (that have no reason – or space – being in the bedrooms) being in the common area, but only if those items don't get in the way of everyone else.

What if a family member decides to put something really big that obstructs the other's way right in the middle of the living room and then keep it there? That wouldn't be too kind, would it? If they had no other place to put it, then maybe it would be understandable, but not justifiable, at least not for the "keeping-it-there" part. The family should talk about it and resolve it in a way that keeps everyone happy and as comfortable as possible.

So, what CAN you do? Well, the ground rule is kind of the same as the one we have for our personal space: clean after yourself.

Let's go back to John, Terry and Max and their movie night: what did they do after cooking the dish and watching the movie? They cleaned up after themselves: they probably cleaned the area where they ate, then took the plates and cutleries back in the kitchen, washed the dishes and cleaned the kitchen area, at least the parts where there were dirty spots that they had previously produced.

Sometimes, cleaning after ourselves isn't enough though, because the common areas aren't there just for our own things. There is also furniture, maybe a tv, sometimes there are some things that hang on the wall, like paintings or photographs... they are full of things that don't specifically belong to anyone. It's not like after watching a painting on the wall you put it away, right? And when we eat all together, sometimes there is just one person that does the washing-up. Well, the best way to resolve this would be to take turns! You could decide all together how to plan this. For example, Monday nights you clean the dishes, while on Tuesday it's the turn of another family member and so on. In these situations, communication is key.

Tips for House Cleaning

As already mentioned, if you already know how to do all of this, then good for you, but I would still suggest that you look at this list of tips anyways, and if you're unsure of something, you can always come back to it!

- **Routine is key** ⇨ And for this one, guess what do you need? That's right, **you need charts**. That way, you'll know when you should clean your sheets and when you need to set the table.

- **Together is better** ⇨ Sometimes, cleaning is a healthy task to do by yourself, maybe by listening to music. There are other moments where doing it in company is better, **especially if you are still learning** and you need a helping hand to guide you through a specific chore.

- **One Step at a Time** ⇨ If you look at a messy room or a big pile of dishes, sometimes you feel like everything it's too overwhelming and you don't know where and how to start tidying. That's where this rule comes in handy. If you are washing the dishes with an adult, start by picking up one thing, think about what you need to do and then do it, slowly and analyzing what you are doing. Sooner than later, the pile of dishes is going to get smaller and smaller, and it won't look that scary anymore. Same thing with a messy room: just **start with one simple corner and then go from there.** The room will be all tidied up in no time.

- **Everything in its right place** ⇨ There is a place for every little thing: **find it and label it**. If you don't want to actually label it, just rename it in your own mind: that drawer is now the "pencils' drawer", and so on. The next time you will clean up, you will know where to put everything.

- **Learn how to do the laundry, mop the floors and vacuum** ⇨ there is no rush really, one step at a time. Always ask for help with these things. They can become dangerous if you don't know how to do them.

- **The trash belongs... well, in the trash**

- **Stay consistent** ⇨ The more you follow your charts, the less you'll have to deal with cleaning and tidying.

- **Celebrate your achievements** ⇨ Every new thing you learn, every new habit you learn, every time you will manage to clean something, **be proud of yourself**! You did it!

Chapter 6: Preparation for the Future

You probably have already finished elementary school, and if not, you are at the very end of it. There isn't really any rush, but it would be best for you to start actually thinking of what you want your future to look like.

When I was a kid, I wanted to become a chef, then I wanted to become a marine biologist and then I wanted to become a doctor. So many different things, but I ended up doing something completely different.

This doesn't mean that I gave up on my dreams, and neither that I was lost in all those different areas and specialties. Life is complicated, sometimes you think you have got it, but something comes out of the blue that makes you reconsider everything. This might feel scary, but that's actually one of the best things about living: you can't control everything!

Some people know what they want to be when they grow up right from the start, and some of them keep having the same dream after they have grown up. Some of them even succeed and turn out to have that job that they were dreaming of having since childhood.

Some other people don't know what they want from the future, there are so many professions, so many choices, and they don't feel like they are ready for what may come. This is absolutely normal and as valid as the previous example. You shouldn't have your whole life figured out already.

What you should and can do, is to work on your strength, and if you don't know which ones they are, start looking for them! Find out what your main interests are and work out whether they can become actual jobs, and before that whether you can study them.

I'll tell you some little fun facts about John and Terry: John is pretty sure of what he wants to become: he wants to be a journalist, so he is now looking into which school to attend after high-school. Terry isn't really sure, but he loves woodworking and discovered that you can study to do that as a job!

This could be a fun experience, let's start!

Why is This Topic So Important?

Whether you already know what you want to do in your life or you have no idea about it, there are many ways to explore the different options you may have in front of you.

You should start now because this could also affect your high-school experience and your decisions in the future.

Again, nothing is set in stone, you have time to change your mind, but let's make a list of the different things you could be interested in. Let's also make a list of your strengths and see if you can combine some of this.

For example: you have two columns, one for your interests and one for your abilities. In the first column, you write down that you love reading. Let's now dive into this information a little deeper: which books do you like? Which genres? Are there any common topics? Now, in the other column, you write down that one of your abilities is actually that you have a colorful imagination (it's a real skill, and it's an incredible one to have). Well, this could lead to a third column, which we could call "opportunities". In this column, based on the match we have between one of your interests and one of your abilities, you could write down many different types of careers. You could become a journalist, a writer, a critic, a librarian... just to name a few! What if you don't feel too sure about your writing skills? This shouldn't stop you, because right after the third column we can add a fourth one with the different studies you can get into in the future. A lot of them are focused on specific areas of the art of language, such as "creative writing" courses, but also "literary study" courses as well!

See? There are so many courses you could attend and just by trying to mix up your strength and abilities.

It can be a fun exercise, but it's also something that could push you towards the realization of what you really want.

Look at it this way, if at first you don't find anything, at least you will know what you don't want to do, which is a great first step if you ask me.

Tips for Career Searching

You can (and should) follow these steps with an adult family member that could guide you through them.

- **Charts** ⇨ This is the thing we just talked about in the previous chapter: prepare your chart with three to four columns, each designated to "interests", "abilities/strengths", "possible careers/studies". Let's focus on each of them and see what they mean. **The interests you have in your daily life might become passions**. Maybe you scribble on your papers when you are absent-minded and drawing turns out to be a hobby. Don't focus on how good you are with your passions, there is always room to grow. Your abilities and strengths might come from many different things: they could be character traits, physical traits, social skills or general ones, like being good at a specific subject in school. The different career options come from how you can combine your strengths and interests, or from just one of the two. The "studies" column is the fourth one because it's the culmination of everything we linked in the previous ones.

- **Be Open-Minded** ⇨ Sometimes these lists don't come easy. When someone asks me something like "what is your favorite movie?" My mind goes completely blank and I can't think of any movie I watched ever, even if I love movies. If you sit down to start filling out the chart and nothing comes out, don't panic. Don't think about it, do something else for a couple of hours and then **you'll discover that the answer will pop-up in your brain during the less predictable moments**. If you have the answers but not the chart with you, write down the discovery wherever you can and copy it on the chart as soon as you can.

- **Watch Movies** ⇨ And television too, for that matter. Sometimes we watch movies and see someone in a job field. We start to feel like that career doesn't seem that bad, and then we grow an interest in that. Be careful though, because the media can sometimes be toxic and have a negative influence on us. Maybe ask an adult family member to do some movie nights with you.

- **Dream Big** ⇨ Right now, **the sky's the limit**. Why shouldn't it be?

Tools for Career Searching

Here are some tools you could use to have some actual practical view and maybe experience of what a career in a specific field could look like. Remember to always take big decisions with the help of the adults that take care of you.

- **Use you Newly-Found Skills** ⇨ Decision-making, Social skills, Critical thinking, Money-Management... everything we talked about in this book could greatly help you in this regard. Learning how to use your skills is empowering, like you had **superpowers**!

- **Volunteer Work** ⇨ This can be searched for in community centers, charity organizations or around your own neighborhood. Like the other practical tools in this list, this could help you grow your social skills, develop more empathy towards others, and see how your work environment is organized. **The first-hand experience is like nothing else**.

- **Workplace Excursion** ⇨ The adults in your family could bring you to their own work and show you how their work-field is like. Some schools do work-field trips as well.

- **Career Counselor** ⇨ With the help of an adult whose profession is literally to help others find the job that most suits them, you could come out of the counseling session with a much **clearer view**.

- **School Activities** ⇨ Some schools provide their students with work-related activities: if your school does something like this, you should really look into it.
- **Part-Time Job** ⇨ If you are old enough, you could always look into a part-time job to do. This could be a good work experience but also a way to gain your own money

Leadership and Teamwork Skills

Almost all careers require you to have good leadership techniques and if not, at least good teamwork abilities.

Being a leader means being in charge of a project, of a work group, of the outcome of an operation. Being a leader can be tough but very rewarding, and the same goes for being a teamplayer: being an active part of a team is a learning process and we are going to start from this chapter.

These are great skills to have, even if we are just talking in general.

Sometimes we learn these skills while being with our friends too.

Let's look at John, Terry and Max again: as already said, Max is a very chill person, they usually go with the flow of things and are very kind towards others. John and Terry have strong personalities and they sometimes butt heads with one another. This is normal and can happen in any kind of relationship dynamic. What's important is how they work through it: they have learned to communicate with one another and have an innate respect for each other, so talking comes easy (especially after the sandwich episode). There isn't really a "leader" in their group, because they are usually able to decide on things together, and none of them have ever taken charge. This is neither a good or a bad thing: it's something that relates more to how their characters are and how they work together. For example, Terry is mellow with their close friends, but could easily take the leadership role and speak up in the name of the rest of the group when faced with problems. If other kids try to bully them, Terry is the first one to protect the others and speaks for the three of them, even if nobody asked him to. This isn't necessarily limited to leadership roles, but it can be a part of it.

Whilst deciding something, for example how to spend the afternoon or the topic of a certain school project, they all share their thoughts and then decide what to do based on everyone's opinion, although it's important to mention that, when Max speaks, every single person listens carefully. Max, being a quiet, chill person, doesn't talk too much unless they are talked to, but that doesn't make their opinion matter less, quite the opposite actually. When Max speaks, it means that they have an opinion that they want to share, and most of the time it's a very introspective and interesting one. Being quiet, shy or chill doesn't mean weak.

These are all things that a member of a team or a leader must understand and take into consideration.

Tips for Leadership and Teamwork Skills

Remember that a work team is different from a friend group. This doesn't mean that you can't be friends with your colleagues, it just means that there is a time and a place for everything. Same thing applies to school actually.

I made a lot of friends in the different places I worked at, but we didn't do friend's activities at work, nor we talked like we would outside of work during working hours.

Anyways, here are some tips:

- **Communication** is ALWAYS key

- **Emotions** should come in the way, but not in the way you may think: emotional intelligence is important in teamwork, and we talked about it in the empathy chapters.
- **Soft skills** at work, like critical thinking, problem solving and decision-making. The more you use them, the more people will trust you and see you as a responsible person they can rely on.
- **Sense of community** is crucial, otherwise there isn't really a team, is there?
- **Let everyone talk**, because each voice is essential and interesting to listen to. Everyone deserves to have the right to speak up.
- **Celebrate each other's successes**, because if team efforts lead to positive results, everyone is to be credited for it. There's no room for jealousy in a team.
- **Admit when you are wrong**.
- **Respect** is and always will be a priority.
- **Set common goals**.
- **We're all in this together**: a team is a team because of circumstances, because of common goals or for many different reasons. What's important is that a team is a close group of people that has to work together, so why not appreciate the value of this?
- **Be honest**, because being honest is a sign of respect. You aren't above anyone else (even when you are a leader)

The Benefits of Teamwork

Lastly, here is a list of positive effects of being a good team-player: always remember that there's no "I" in "team", which basically means that there's no room for arrogance or egoism in the workplace, this applies to friend groups too. Notice that there's no "I" in "leader" as well? That's because even if in a position of power, the main focus should be the group you are working for, its wellness and its productivity. Everyone has to do their own part, and no one has to feel like all the burden of the work lands on their shoulders, not even the leader.

- **No Conflict** ⇨ If a team is well managed, communication shouldn't be a problem. **Conflicts can and will happen nonetheless, because it's normal human behavior**. However, with a well-oiled team, conflict-resolutions will come no problem, the communication between different team members will always be key.

- **Working on the same goal** ⇨ You will all feel like you are a part of same community: that's because you all kind of are! As part of the same group, you will have similar goals, or even the same one! Just like in school, when you have to do a group project: you will have to partake in the work if you want to get good results, and **it is way better if everyone feels involved**.

- **More Productivity** ⇨ If everyone feels involved, everyone will want to strive to succeed. This means that you will work harder and faster, you will do a better job and much more free time on your hands as well. **Good teamwork and productivity benefit everyone**.

- **Obstacles don't look too hard to overcome** ⇨ Just like you would in a sport team, when you feel like there is a common problem, when you aren't doing the best you could, if there is that famous sense of community, you won't see those problems as impossible and overwhelming.

- **Trust** ⇨ You will be able to trust each other, and vice versa.
- **Less Stress** ⇨ As already mentioned, more productivity, more free time!

Chapter 7: Health and Wellness

Being a tween is hard. It just is, and sometimes teenage years are hard too. This isn't because of some character flaw or anything like that, it actually has a scientific reason. The reason being something that we already mentioned in the previous chapters: brain-development. Since your brain is now evolving at full speed, and probably your body as well, confusion and strong, seemingly uncontrollable emotions are normal and to be expected.

Something that it's also important to remember is that everyone grows at their own rhythm: some develop early and some much later in life, don't let this define you or anyone in your life. It's not like you're worse or better than someone if you developed early: this is just how bodies work, there's really nothing else to it. Most of the mocking and bullying, objectifying and insulting behavior that stems from this particular subject come from insecurity, and that's just sad. If you feel like you are being mocked for your appearance, the best thing you could do would be to talk to someone about it, but if you don't feel like you're ready to communicate about this, you need to try to ignore them, because bullies or just insecure people feed from the other people's attention. That's what I did when I was young and being picked on because of my height. I was a bit short, but it honestly could have been anything, from acne, to having long arms or a bigger neck... anything that involved looking a little bit odd could have triggered my insecure classmates to pick on me. I stuck to my plan and just completely ignored them. They did everything they could to get a reaction from me, but sooner or later I realized that if I did get angry or frustrated (at least in front of them) I would have played their own game, and I knew I was better than that. I still got sad and upset, but those feelings went away once and for all once I learned my actual worth, which was automatically superior to the one of someone that needs to bring other people down to make themselves feel better. That's what I did, and it helped me, but it's possible that it's not the best solution for you. I did what I did out of survival instincts kicking in, and maybe out of being more mature than my bullies.

As I said, the best thing you could do is to speak up. This doesn't make you look like them, because you're not insulting them: you are defending yourself, and those are two incredibly different things.

Nothing that it's going on in your body and mind is your fault.

Healthy Eating Habits

How you eat influences you in the long run: you also need to have a healthy relationship with your own body. This is crucial, both for your physical and mental health. If you think that you don't have a good relationship with food, please seek the help of a professional. Unhealthy eating habits could come from many different situations, but what's important is how to unlearn them and to eat in a happy and healthy way.

This goes beyond the basic rules of what you shouldn't do, for example "too much sugar will give you a fast, high-energy peak and a very low energy level right after", or "if you eat too much junk food you will have a stomach ache". As previously mentioned, these tips are more focused on your healthy habits in the long run. Will you be able to be independent with your own food-making process and meal prepping once you are older? Do you know what it means to eat in a healthy way?

And the answer isn't necessarily "eat a lot of veggies and avoid junk food", although these are good points too. Look, if you want to eat junk food once in a while, that's fine. It's when you consume them once or even twice a day that it becomes an issue. You should be able to enjoy the food you love whenever you want, but not if that specific food isn't healthy for you. I love fries, hell, I would love anything if it's fried enough. I don't eat them everyday though, because that would be nonsensical of me to do so! I don't even eat them once a week. What I do is wait maybe two to three weeks and then treat myself to a nice plate of fries, or to a nice fried dish. By doing this, not only do I prioritize my health, but fries and fried stuff in general have become some sort of prize. If I was to discover that, for some health reason, I wouldn't be able to eat fried stuff anymore... sure, I would be upset at first, but I care about myself and my well-being too much not to shrug this off. There are so many incredibly tasty healthy alternatives to unhealthy foods!

Eating junk-food regularly doesn't only affect your health, but also your mood.

Tips for Healthier Eating Habits

These are things you could introduce to your day-to-day life that could help you grow healthy food habits. This kind of advice is very general: sometimes people have allergies, sometimes they have dietary restrictions, so be careful and apply these tips as needed.

- **Don't force yourself** ⇨ You shouldn't feel like you have to eat everything that's on your plate if you feel too full, you shouldn't feel judged, (even by yourself) if you feel like you need to go for seconds: you're still growing, your body is developing. Please, **be kind to yourself. Eat what you feel like**, listen to yourself, don't judge yourself.

- **Try to eat three times a day** ⇨ You should at least eat three times a day: **breakfast, lunch and dinner**. There are many different ideas on how much you should eat for each meal, just follow whatever your family's habits are, I'm sure they know better. If you want to be sure yourself, go ahead and ask them the reasons why of your food habits. Being curious is always a good thing, but remember to do it in a respectful manner.

- **Eat snacks** ⇨ If you feel hungry outside of the three meals, **you should be able to snack**. Snacking isn't necessarily unhealthy, on the contrary: there are so many snacking habits that are both good for you and that imply ingesting healthy foods.

- **Eat as healthy as possible** ⇨ As previously mentioned, there are a lot of healthy foods you could eat or decide to eat. If you are interested, ask someone to help you research.

- **Try to avoid mixing eating with screen-time** ⇨ This is just because it leads to something that can be called "**passive eating**". You focus more of your attention on the screen you are looking at, (whether it's a phone, a tablet, a computer or a tv screen) and less on the food you are eating. This can lead to eating too much or far less than you should. The most important thing you could do is to learn to listen to your own body, it tells you what it needs.

- **Avoid sugary foods before bed** ⇨ And energy drinks in general, for that matter. If your energy levels run high, sleeping becomes far less easy, and if you aren't able to sleep, your sleeping cycle becomes far less healthy. We are going to talk about sleep-hygiene in the next chapters.

Physical Exercise

One of the topics we previously mentioned but didn't analyze, was how crucial physical exercise is in our day-to-day life, not only for your body and your growth, but also for your mental health and well-being.

Sometimes we go through rough times in life, it happens and that's ok, what we need to focus on is how to deal with them, exactly as if someone in our life hurt us or has brought us down in some way: we can't control what other people do or say, what we can control though, is how to respond to a certain situation. Rough times, stress, and negative emotions must not rule our lives. One thing we can do to help us is this: exercise!

If you are unsure whether doing exercises is good or bad for you, think of it this way: there can be two situations in life.

The first one: you are happy and having a good time. Everything (or almost everything) is good, life is good. There are some things to handle, but it's fine, you know you can do it. So, generally, all is well.

The second one: you are experiencing a rough situation, and negative emotions aren't so easy to handle. It seems that everything is going wrong. This happens all the time when you are experiencing a bad moment: it seems like an avalanche is running down a mountain, the faster it runs, the bigger it gets. Most of the time it's just an illusion, but it doesn't feel quite like it in our own head.

Well, if you think about it, both these life situations are good to exercise in! For the first one, it would help you focus, stay positive, release energy in a positive way and overall keep you healthy. For the second one, exercise could be the helping hand you may need from yourself. It could help you remind yourself how strong and incredible you are, how capable and strong you can be when needed.

I don't see any cons in these two options, do you?

I invite you to try keeping the habit of physical exercise: if you try one and you don't like it, if you don't feel like it suits you, go on and try the next one! There are so many different sports you could try!

If you are curious, John does archery, Terry is a swimmer and Max is a great fencer and volleyball player!

Tips for Introducing Sports and Exercises into your Habits

It really depends on your day-to-day schedule, because there are many people that fit sports into their schedule depending on their other obligations and responsibilities: some do them early in the morning before starting school or work, some do them after school or work, and some practice them during the evening. It also depends on the sport itself: for example, some sports can't be practiced in the evening.

These are some of the tips:

- **Sports can be fun** ⇨ They can become a great way of having fun while also doing something good for yourself. It really depends on what you like, but **you should have fun** whilst practicing!

- **Sports can be done alone or in a team** ⇨ **Sportsmanship** is very important in life, but I understand that not all people are fond of practicing team sports, for instance, I enjoy practicing sports by myself, but **this is completely up to you** and what you prefer.

- **Sports can relieve stress** ⇨ If you are experiencing a busy moment in your life, practicing could be a great way for **pausing your life and focusing on what you are doing in that moment**. For example, imagine living in a very loud environment, and then going swimming. Suddenly, you are immersed in a world of peace and silence and your only focus is doing laps and feeling the water on your skin. Even while pushing yourself, you feel at peace. Cool, right?

- **Sports can be of a great variety** ⇨ Sports can be done while practicing with **your own body** (swimming, dancing, running), while **using an object** of some sort (archery, fencing, pole vaulting), while **using a ball** (soccer, tennis, basket) ... seriously, these are the first examples that popped in my head, but there are so many!

- **Sports can be done in many locations** ⇨ Swimming pools, fields, at home...

- **Sports can be artistic** ⇨ Some may say that all sports have an artistic part in and of themselves, but some of them are described as art forms in general, such as dancing. If you like to express yourself through art, you have the possibility to merge sports and your desire for arts into one thing.

Sleep Hygiene and Mental Health

Some people think that sleeping is a waste of time, because you could use those few hours to do what needs to be done. I know that, in my teenage years, I used to go to sleep very late, because night time was the best time for me to study. Not because I didn't have enough time during the day, but because my brain felt more active during those hours. I knew that it wasn't healthy for me but I did it anyway, that led me to having bigger sleeping problems later in life, because by falling asleep during the middle of the night and having to wake up early messed with my circadian rhythm.

But what is a circadian rhythm? Imagine having a clock inside of your body. That clock works in the background of your life and has its own rhythms, the most famous one being the cycle that makes you fall asleep at night and wake up in the morning. We are animals, and as such, we have some cool "powers" that come from our ancestors: for example, did you know that, for most of us, green is the color of which we see the highest number of shades? That's because our ancestors lived in a world full of nature, a lot more nature than now, and they were also considered a prey for bigger animals. They needed to be able to focus whilst in the forest, or else they would become someone else's meal. For this reason, their eyes developed in such a way that they were able to see so many different types of green that they could actually notice animals that were camouflaging themselves in the woods. Something else we took after our ancestor was the fact that we can't really shut one of our senses off: our hearing. We can shut our eyes, avoid touching or tasting something by staying away from it and closing our mouths, we can pinch our nose and... well, you could make a point that you can stick a finger in each ear and stop hearing, but that would not be true, not in the literal sense at least. Our ears are designed to hear even when shut: that's because our ancestors, as preys, had to make sure they could run away when hearing a predator coming, even when we were sleeping.

So, there you go, this is one of the reasons why our bodies work better when following the day/night cycle. That's why we should sleep a certain amount of hours in order to feel awake and active the next day, and that's why sleeping the right amount of hours but during odd hours, such as from the middle of the night to midday, isn't the same as falling asleep in the evening and waking up in the morning.

Why is Sleeping So Important?

The amount of sleep you need varies depending on one's age group. Your need for sleep slightly lessens once you grow older, but there really isn't a great difference. At your age, it's usually recommended to sleep somewhere from 10 to 13 hours a day, including naps.

Not all of us enjoy napping though, so that's up to you. Of course, we must when we are very little, but napping can also mean just resting and turning your mind off for some time. Some people love napping, even when older, and feel absolutely energized and ready to go after taking them, but that's not how everyone's bodies work. I know some people that hate how they feel after a nap. Taking naps should be relaxing and energizing, so maybe try a few methods before deciding if they are good for you or not. Sometimes, the duration of the nap is crucial. What's important is how you spend your time instead of napping: that's the designated time for you to rest, not to distress or to have some extra fun with adrenaline-filled activities. You should stay in a dark room with something that you know makes you relax, whether it's a book or some music... something to help you feel like you were napping without actually napping. This works only if napping isn't for you, because otherwise you should continue doing it.

Sleeping the right number of hours, at the right time and in the right conditions helps us greatly, not only to be our most energetic selves: going without any of those three elements (hours, time, conditions), for a long amount of time could hurt us in the long run. For example, if someone has anxiety and has a messed up sleeping cycle for any of the above reasons, it is more likely that the anxiety will grow and become more unmanageable. Sleeping directly affects our mental health, if we sleep well, there are more possibilities of us helping ourselves and our own health.

In the next chapter, there will be tips on how to effectively help our sleeping cycle and sleep hygiene.

Strategies for Introducing Good Sleeping Habits in Your Life

- **Less Blue Light Before Sleeping** ⇨ Blue light is the one that comes from any technological device. It can come from your phone, tablet, computer or television. The problem with blue light before sleeping is that it tricks your brain into believing that it's daytime, it riles it up and gives you an adrenaline rush, like your body does when it wakes up. Even if it feels like it relaxes you and makes you sleepy, the reality is that it really doesn't: **how you sleep with or without screen-time beforehand affects the quality of the sleep itself.**

- **No Sugar/Energy-inducing food or beverages before bed** ⇨ As already mentioned, this habit isn't ideal and is actually unhealthy. Not only does it increase the possibility of stomach aches at night, but it can also make oneself have that famous **rush of adrenaline that won't help you fall asleep** any faster. A big meal before bed is also discouraged as a habit, as it can sometimes lead to a difficult sleeping situation, including nightmares.

- **Regulate naps/Resting time** ⇨ If you nap too much during the day, you won't feel sleepy enough to go to bed at the designated time. It's just logic.

- **Sleep schedule** ⇨ Don't worry, I'm not asking you to make another chart. This is more like an unwritten rule. You decide that, for example, you want to go to bed at 9 p.m., so that you can get a full 10, 11 hours of sleep and wake up at the right time to go to school or do what you need to. That's it. There is a catch though: you have to stick to this rule as much as you can. **Be dedicated and your circadian rhythm will thank you**.

- **Surrounding environment** ⇨ If you have too much light coming in the bedroom from the window, too many lights in the room, too much noise... it could lead to insomnia or a bad night of sleep. You need to have control of your environment before going to bed, so that it can be as relaxing as possible. Some people like to fall asleep with white noises or relaxing music, some like for it to be completely silent. Some like to have some sort of light next to their bed, some don't. You decide.

- **Bath or shower before bed/Physical exercise** are both great ways of relaxing and falling asleep easier. If you exercise, **your body is tired and relaxes easily**, if you take a bath before going to bed, not only it helps your muscles, but it can really make you more comfortable and ready to get some good solid sleep.

Environmental Awareness and Sustainability

Imagine that the whole world is the house that you live in.

Now, imagine that there are many people that come and go from your house: some are very polite and keep everything clean and in order, it's like they never popped by. Some other people are rude, they don't clean after themselves and litter, they leave their trash everywhere and are just plain impolite, they act like they are the only ones living in your own house. They leave all the lights on and play loud music anytime they want. They drink all your water and eat your food. When they don't finish your food, they just throw the rest of it anywhere they feel like. Every corner of your house is dirty, littered with trash and overall disgusting. It seems that it doesn't make a difference whether the polite people stop by or not. Some of them stay a bit more just to help you clean around, but they can only do so much, when the rude ones keep coming and do what they do. When you try to ask rude people to stop their behavior, they usually have two to three universal answers. The first one is: "well, this isn't my place, I don't have responsibilities over it because I don't own it, so I don't care". The second one is: "Well, I understand, but others do much worse than me and I don't see you talking to them. Also, I see that some people are helping you clean everything up, so there you go.". The third one is just ignoring you until you get sick and tired of pressuring them and go away.

The sad part is that this isn't a made-up scenario. Don't worry, your house is not going to get flooded with people destroying it, let's reverse the first sentence. The world is not your house, but your house is the world. Everything you can look at when walking through a city, a park, the beach, the sea... everything is the responsibility of everyone. Some people use their free time to go clean the beaches because of how bad people treat them.

Nothing must be taken for granted. The world isn't fixed, the sea won't clean itself and neither will most of the trash that doesn't go in its designated bins. We all have to think of the world as a gifted, incredible home that has to be taken care of, and this is our highest responsibility. You may think "what is the difference if I do something? I'm only one person". That's the beauty of it. Could you imagine if every single person in your neighborhood decided to treat the world as their home? The environmental change would be incredible! Now, imagine if everyone in the world took their own responsibility seriously. Imagine if everyone did their own part for our common home. What a change, huh?

How to Help the Environment

This book already contains many different topics, it would take an entire other book just about this one to dive into it at its fullest. The tips I'm going to give you are very general, and most certainly aren't the only things you can do to help. I ask you to get interested in this topic, if you aren't already. Do some research if you can. It's something we can all do and partake in.

- **Precycle, Recycle, Upcycle!** ⇨ **Precycle** = essentially buying something, knowing how much will you be able to use the product, how much of it you will be able to recycle and if it's worth it. **Recycle** = if you throw all the used plastic away in one place, it will be easier to transform it into something new. **Upcycle** = taking something that could have been thrown in the trash and turning it into something new. A pair of old jeans that doesn't fit you anymore can turn into a bag, or many other things. By transforming something that isn't usable anymore, you have made something new that can be used for much longer.

- **Don't waste products** ⇨ Even when you feel like you have used something at its fullest, **there are still things that could be done**. An old t-shirt that you used until you couldn't and that had become something you wore only when you knew you would get dirty, can become a rag. That bottle of shampoo can still contain some of it: add some water and mix everything up, so that it can still be used for a couple more showers.

- **Don't take too long in the shower** ⇨ The less water we waste, the more environment-friendly we become.

- **Turn off your devices when you are not using them**.

- **Walk or use a bike whenever possible**.

- **Don't litter**

- **Care!** ⇨ By spreading the word, more and more people will become part of the helping hand that the world needs. Teach others, volunteer, help however you can!

Chapter 8: Digital Skills

The Internet can be an incredible place. It is full of information: from world-wide news (get it?) to social media, to tips about anything and everything, to forums where you can find like-minded people to talk to about your shared interests.

Sometimes, the internet can make you feel like a better person. It can keep you updated on your any interest, it can help you support any cause, it can lead you to new worlds and make you become a whole lot more open-minded, especially if you live in a secluded part of the world or if you are particularly privileged. It can expand your horizons and it can also be the place where you search and find jobs. And to think that it was officially invented in 1983! This is the umpteenth proof that technology is a fast-growing reality, now more than ever. It only took some years for it to become an essential part of our life. In some ways, it's for the best.

In some ways, it can be daunting. Think about it: anyone can write what they want on the internet. Anyone, anywhere. For as much information, socialization, support and open-mindedness you can get, you receive as much possible danger. The internet can become a scary place and people can get physically and mentally hurt from it. The internet is like a digitalization of our world, and our world is full of both good and bad people, the only difference being that on the internet people feel like they can say anything to you, even when you don't know them, just because they can, just because they don't have to face you. People can try to con you, they can try to get your personal information, they feel omnipotent, just because they have the power of the internet.

It's kind of like when two dogs start furiously barking at each other, have you seen the videos? Sometimes, they even have to be held, because they act like they would get in a fight if not. Then, one or both of the dogs get set free, they are now close to each other, with no human nor glass wall between them. They suddenly stop barking and avoid each other's eye-contact, almost in an awkward way. If they get to be held back again, they start the barking once more.

How to be Safe and Responsible on the Internet

The first thing you need to learn is that everything, and I mean everything you post on the internet is there forever. Even if you think you have deleted it, it's still there, somewhere. I won't even put this in the usual advice-section we have for each chapter, because it's not even an advice, it's a basic rule that everyone that surfs the internet must know and must remember. It's not like you have to be scared to post anything, you just have to remember something called "digital footprint".

Do you remember when we talked about critical thinking and I asked you to pretend that you were a detective? Well, it's time to do it again.

So, detective, there is a crime to solve. This crime was committed somewhere in the city, but we obviously don't know who has done it! What we need to do is trace their steps, right? So, we go to the crime scene and find out that the criminal had left footprints all over the location, we follow them to a café, where we manage to gather some information about how long the criminal stayed there, what they eat and drink and if they paid or not. We then chat with the bartender and ask them questions about the criminal: it turns out that they took a picture of them because they thought the criminal looked suspicious (and they were right), so then we go around with the picture, asking if someone has seen that face before. Meanwhile, our colleague who is still at the crime scene has found some footprints and has talked to the people that live in the area and found some interesting links to our crime. We go back to the scene with the picture of the criminal and we show it to the person who has given us more information. We now know a lot more, most importantly, we know where the criminal is heading, because someone that had seen the picture we have, recognized the person and told us that the culprit hopped on the first available taxi and was going to the airport. We arrived there just in time before the plane took off.

The lawbreaker was lazy and had left us a trail of footprints all over the place. They were recognizable, and even if they were innocent, it took a very short time for us to trace their steps back.

This is what a digital footprint is about: we all leave a trace of where we went in the digital world, and we have to at least acknowledge how powerful that information could be if it got in the wrong hands.

Most of us are guilt-free, and it's not like you need to be a criminal to care about your footprints: you have to care about those even if you are the detective, even if you are an innocent bystander.

Online Safety Tips and Guidelines

- **Don't share personal information online** ⇨ Some people may use it against you. Have you ever heard of something called "doxing"? It's when people share addresses, personal numbers and information of someone else online and without their permission. This could lead to a bunch of different problems and to danger, so **make sure to keep all of your personal information to yourself**. Never, under any circumstance, post them online for anyone to see.

- **Don't accept candy from strangers** ⇨ This is something that was already taught you sooner in life, and it applies to the internet too. **Don't talk to people you don't know, don't decide to meet with them, don't trust them**. People can be very nasty sometimes, and you can't put your own safety in the hands of someone you don't know in real life or that you have never met. Sometimes people catfish, meaning that they pretend to be other people to lure you in. If you feel like a conversation that you've had online with someone you think you know doesn't feel safe or gives you a bad feeling, take a step back and try to understand whether you are actually talking to the right person online. Tell the adults in your house about this and maybe, next time you meet this person in real life, ask about that conversation you had online. Identity theft is a serious crime.

- **Adult's permission** ⇨ As you are far from being an adult, you need one to ask permission to, at least for some things. One being the access to some things, both online and in real life. There is a reason why some sites aren't for minors to go through, same reason why you aren't allowed to drive or to drink: it could be dangerous.

- **Don't post** ⇨ Not in general, but as previously mentioned, your digital footprint is there, something that seems private can look like it but may not be it, some things seem safe to post but they aren't. Whether you are new to the internet world or not, you should ask for an adult's opinion before posting something, anything.

- **Don't click or download anything without being sure of it** ⇨ Internet viruses are very real. As much as I enjoy the picture of a computer sneezing and having a fever, a virus is something that could shut your internet devices in a second. They are intelligent and could be hidden anywhere. In order to be safe on the internet, you must be aware of these possibilities. It gets easier with practice, once you've been on the internet long enough you tend to recognize certain patterns: it could be a weird message on social media, it could be an email with a link attachment, it could be a funny titled video with a big download sign under it. You never know.

- **If you are uncomfortable, run** ⇨ Whether you're chatting with someone, surfing random sites and stumble upon something weird, browsing social media and see a strange video, the answer is always one: log off, stay away from it. This isn't "tween advice", it's "general life" advice. You know that saying? "It's like a car crash, you can't look away", well, it's both true and untrue. You do feel like you need to keep watching if you stumble upon something horrible, but you still have the power over yourself to look away. No one is forcing you to keep looking or keep searching, and our gut feeling is almost always correct. If you ever have a wary feeling about something while being online, please stop whatever it is that you are doing and step away.

- **Create strong passwords and change them from time to time** ⇨ It's like when you have to close something with a lock: you don't want to have 000 on your lock as your code, right? That would be too easy to crack. Usually, the sites that require a password guide you on how to make the perfect one, but don't forget it! Write the password down on a piece of paper and keep it safe.

- **Don't trust the internet** ⇨ anyone can write anything they want about any subject.

Cyberbullying and Social-Media

I hope you never have to experience anything like it, but if you decide to have an online-profile on social media, you need to know this. Cyberbullying is a dangerous reality, it's scary and stressful. You need to make yourself your number one priority, your mental and physical health are the most important things in your life. We've previously talked about bullies whilst talking about conflict resolution and mental health awareness.

Cyberbullying is incredibly dangerous, because it's relentless, cruel and doesn't have boundaries. There isn't a comparison to be made between bullies that you have to deal with face-to-face and bullies online: they are both terrible and have to be stopped.

The real difference is that cyberbullying is easier for the bullies themselves, because they can hide behind their screens, it has a much bigger pool of people that can watch and partake in the bullying (random videos can go viral in just a few hours) and lastly, as previously mentioned, it knows no boundaries. It feels like it follows you everywhere you go, even where you feel physically safe.

The answer is never to become a bully yourself, and always to be the bigger person. Ask for help any way you can, put your trust in the right people, block and report the people that are hurting you. This is something that must be taken seriously. Remember the guidelines from the previous chapter and stick to them, don't share personal information, remember that, in most places, it is illegal to share videos or pictures without one's consent, especially if you are a minor.

You are never alone, there is always a way to ask for help.

Fake News and Online Scams

The world is riddled with people that think they know everything. Sometimes they go to the doctor because they've read that their headache could be the symptom of terrible diseases, and how did they come to that conclusion? They read it on the internet. Sometimes they wholeheartedly hate someone (famous or not) because they think they did something terrible. They read it on the internet. Sometimes they assure you that they know something more than you, even if it's something that you are an expert in, because guess what? They read something on the internet.

People trust too much what they read online. Sometimes, because of this gullibility, they get scammed.

There are many ways for someone to get scammed online. Most of the time, they revolve around money. You may think you are giving money for a game, for a cause, for funding something, while in reality you are getting scammed, your money isn't going where you think it is and on top of it all, from this exchange, the scammers could grab your personal information.

It is important to have control of what you are doing online, to be able to recognize a scam before getting trapped into it or to identify fake news before it is fed to you.

The worst thing is that you could partake in the misinformation if you aren't careful enough.

In the next chapter, we will dive into some of the actions you can take and some tips to stay safe online.

Tips on How to Identify and Protect Yourself from Fake News and Online Scams

- **Think before sharing** ⇨ If you aren't sure of an information, don't hit the share button. This is how misinformation spreads. There are many ways to fact-check what you see and read, so before putting all your eggs in one basket, take a step back. Remind yourself that there isn't any rush and **prioritize checking whether that piece of information is plausible and, most of all, correct.**

- **Check the source** ⇨ Always check the source. Did someone send you the information? On what social media or site are you on? Check the account that is sharing that information, most of the time it's not too hard to identify fake accounts. Take a look at them and compare them to your own, see if it shares a lot of links, ask yourself if it is a credible source.

- **Always be aware of the context in which specific information is shared**.

- **Don't trust the comment section** ⇨ Don't trust pop-up ads either. While looking at a video and wondering "is this true?", looking at what other people think isn't a good fact-checking technique. There are many gullible people that feed from whatever they read, they also feel the need to comment on it and on other people's content as well. Everyone is entitled to their own opinion, but it doesn't make it right to share it, if you aren't sure of the source. You wouldn't put out a comment spurring negative thoughts about a movie if you haven't seen it, right? It wouldn't make sense. Imagine if I want to watch that movie, but I see your comment online and think otherwise just because I trusted that comment. And you didn't even see it!

- **Don't use social media as your news source** ⇨ If you want to go to the internet to search for news, or if you are on social media and see some news you are interested in, don't click on it. Go to a trusted news site and look for it. News on social media is almost always biased. Find a news' site you feel like you can trust and that looks as official and unbiased as possible. This is also a source of misinformation: what if someone that really dislikes a famous person decides to share some news about them but, while doing so, putting a negative twist, changing the context, anything to make them look bad? What if other people see this information, believe in it and share it?

- **Use a safe Wi-Fi connection**, don't trust the ones without authentication. They could be a bait, and dangerous for your own devices.

- **Don't open links if you aren't sure of them.**

- **Stay on official gaming platforms.**

- **Always take things with a grain of salt**.

How to Do Research Online

Not so long ago, kids had to go to the library and use encyclopedias and dictionaries to grab the information they needed. There literally wasn't any other possible source of information that they could use or study from.

When the internet came around, all you needed to do was grab a computer, type the topic you had to research and boom, loads and loads of information, right there.

As we now know though, there are many risks to surf the internet freely, most of the time being online directly correlates to being exposed to misinformation. So, how do you do online research?

Actually, some of the tips and advice that were given to you in the previous chapters can be applied here: don't use social media as a news or information source, always check from where the information you are getting comes from and only use official and unbiased platforms.

There also are search engines that are specifically targeted towards minors and that are supposedly child/tween/teenager friendly.

Your first steps into online research should be guided from a trusted adult, say a teacher or an adult family member. Ask for help on what "keywords" are, ask them how to go about it, maybe ask for them to assist you for the first couple of times that you have to do this type of research.

If you need to write down the results of your studies, don't copy and paste from the source: this is considered copying or worse, plagiarism (claim a work as yours when it isn't). Finding out if you copied your information is incredibly easy to do…also it isn't right. Make sure to reformulate the information without losing its concept. If you search on specific sites for your research, there is something called webography: a list of links that lead to the websites you used for your research. It's usually put at the end of the paper.

These are the basics, good luck with your online journey!

Chapter 9: Creative and Artistic Skills

Art is a vast and incredible world, it is full of expression and acceptance. There are as many types of art as you can imagine out there, and people perform them for so many different reasons.

Imagine the world of art as a new planet. You discovered it, now you can explore it if you want.

In this chapter, you are going to be an astronaut, wandering around this new mysterious place full of delightful mysteries. Ready for the lift off, captain?

Now, the first thing that you see on this planet are these huge doors, each with a big number on it. You count the doors and there are 7 of them. You circle around them, but there is nothing behind. It looks like they are magically standing, majestic as they are, firm in their own position, as though gravity didn't exist (you are on a new planet, after all, who knows if gravity exists here?). The good news is that they are unlocked, and you know this because you tried to open a random one and it doesn't oppose resistance, it's like they are waiting for you to open them.

The logical thing to do would be to start from the lowest number, and since they go from 1 to 7, let's open the first one.

And then, magic happens.

As soon as you open the door, you have to protect yourself from the strong wind that hits you. You squint your eyes and you can finally see what's going on. A new world shows up to you, right inside that door. It's only there when you keep the door open, so you use something to block the door open, and you bravely step into the door frame.

These seven doors all contain what are considered as the 7 Fine Arts: Architecture, Sculpture, Painting, Music, Literature, Dance and Cinema.

Although, there are smaller doors all around the planet, and they don't have numbers on them: those are all the other arts that don't fit into the 7 main categories, but they are still as valid.

It could take a lifetime to choose which one to enter, but no worries: there's no rush. I'll keep them open for you.

Expressing Yourself Through Art and Creativity

As we talked about in the intro of this chapter, people dive into arts for a lot of different reasons. These are some of them.

- **Understanding themselves** ⇨ Through art, people have a way of connecting to themselves. Sometimes, we feel lost in our emotions, we don't really understand why we have some of them, sometimes we don't even know what we are feeling. Going for a run or taking a bath and letting your mind wander does the trick for some, but others prefer to try to draw, let their hands roam freely on the paper and find out what they feel through this action. Some need to dance, some need to write something. Performing makes your head run free, it can make it focus on something else other than your confusion or your negative emotions. In the art world, there aren't any rules, not really, so you do what you feel like in the moment and then go from there.

- **Understanding emotions** ⇨ This can be very therapeutic, it makes you more clear-minded, you are able to live the moment without having any immediate worry, so when you finish performing and your mind goes back to how you were feeling before, it is much more organized. It would be like having a messy room and then leaving it as is, go do something else, come back and realize that things are organized again, all clean and tidy. You just had to step away for a while.

- **Self-Expression** ⇨ Everyone has something to say. Each one of us has an art planet in ourselves, we just need to know which door can make us feel just right. Expressing ourselves it's part of the human experience, we are unique, hence we all perform in an original way. There is no room for fear in this, no room for being insecure, because the only significant judgment is the one we have for ourselves.

- **Communication** ⇨ With your own self, with others... communicating your feelings with art is a very healthy way of dealing with emotions or a situation you are dealing with.

- **You just love how art makes you feel, so just do it**.

How to Explore Different Art Forms and Our Own Creativity

- **A miss is a blessing in disguise** ⇨ Don't be scared of doing something wrong: it's from our mistakes that we understand what to do next time around. We just need to be objective with our work (and don't get offended easily) and most importantly, to be patient with ourselves. No one is born knowing everything. You can't become a professional or an expert in something by just reading a book or doing a little research.

- **Be brave** ⇨ I knew someone that told me that she didn't do anything if she knew she would not be the best in it. I have pitied her since her confession. What a sad world if you decide to stay in your own bubble and you are so insecure about yourself that you never try anything new. My point is: don't give up easily.

- **Be truthful to yourself** ⇨ In order to be able to express yourself, you have to accept the truth, as much as you may don't like it. Otherwise, it would be false and counterproductive. Once you arrive to a conclusion, be honest with yourself, accept who you are.

- **Relax** ⇨ Take it easy, do whatever it is that can help you remove some of the stress you may feel. Remember: the only one that has to be happy and satisfied with your art is yourself. That doesn't mean that you don't have to accept criticism: on the contrary. If you receive constructive criticism, you accept it and be humble, look at your art/performance and work from there.

- **Be curious** ⇨ There's no problem if you love the first art form that you have tried so much that you have decided to stick to it, if so, you have some luck on you! To be open-minded and expand our horizon is very important though, and there's no harm in trying something different from time to time, for no other reason than to be curious and explore how much you can, absorb how much you can. So many artists that are famous for one art form have taken inspiration from other art forms in order for them to create more.

- **Take a leap of faith** ⇨ Don't be judgmental, go ahead and try. You never know!

Some of the Different Art Forms that Exist

As previously mentioned, there are the ones considered to be Fine Arts:

- Architecture
- Sculpture
- Painting
- Music
- Literature
- Dance
- Cinema

It's important to note that these have many ramifications in them as well: cinema could mean performing as an actor, being a director, a cinematographer, a set designer... The options are many and all of them can be interesting and crucial in their own way.

Then there are other art forms, such as:

- Photography
- Drawing
- Theatre
- Ceramic art
- Crocheting
- Poetry
- Printmaking
- Decorative arts

- Animation
- Comics
- Digital Art
- Fashion
- Glass art
- Chalk art
- Graphic Design
- Jewelry
- Mixed Media
- Pottery
- Mosaics
- Performance art

And trust me, there are so many more.

Remember that there's always the possibility of attending art classes, both in school or not, there are extra-curricular activities that involve art as well, you could ask your teachers about them. Dance classes, pottery workshops... you name them, they exist! Ask your adult family members about them, so you can search for the right ones together. One other thing you could do is to hang out at places where those art forms are performed, such as museums (if you like paintings) or the theater. That way, you can experience it firsthand and see what it feels like.

Developing Talents and Interests

Sometimes the first step is the hardest one to make, even if it's something we want to do. Maybe because we are scared, maybe because we feel insecure about the outcome, maybe because we don't even know where to start.

Sometimes taking the first step is everything you need to do. Look at how many art forms exist, look at how many possibilities there are out there. The only thing you need to worry about is which one to try first!

The key is: baby steps. Don't rush into things, you have time. One other thing we need to rely on regarding the arts is that it's all based on gut-feeling. There can be no logic to it if you don't want there to be. When I advised you to not give up easily, it doesn't imply that, if you immediately feel uneasy while trying something, you need to keep going. If this situation presents itself, there's no shame in stepping away and finding something else that can work for you. What I mean with my advice, is simply to not overthink things. So what, if you aren't good at it on the first, second or even third try? So what, if you see people do a better job than you?

Terry and Max have the same artistic hobby: they both love photography. This isn't something that John is particularly into, but they don't have to share everything. Terry started practicing his photography skills quite young, whilst Max, on the other hand, is new to this world and isn't as experienced as Terry. This doesn't divide them, nor makes Terry feel like they are better than Max, on the contrary: Max feels comfortable enough to ask Terry questions about it, so much so that they have long discussions about the technical side of it and their different approaches to the art. They talk about which professional photographers they love the most and why. Max has even started mixing two art forms together: photography and graphic design. Terry likes nature photography and they often go on little trips together to take pictures, but the outcome of their art-trips is very different. They could snap the same photo and the finished outcome could be completely different, and they love it.

There is no judgment neither in real friendship nor in art. Even if Max is a beginner, it doesn't get to their head. It makes them strive to learn more and experience the art form as much as they can.

So, the lesson is: don't be afraid, don't give up on the first drawback.

Chapter 10: Cultural and Global Awareness

We are at the last stop of this journey, and here is our last episode of the lives of John, Terry and Max. Only this time, we will go back to the start and only talk about the relationship between John and Terry.

We talked a lot about how their friendship is, what are their interests, their hobbies, their favorite sports, how they resolve their arguments.

What we didn't talk about is the fact that John and Terry come from completely different cultural backgrounds. They live in the same town and attend the same school... They are the best of friends. They have deep cultural differences. Terry has half of his family in another country, the one where his family is from, but Terry feels like he is both from his native country and the one he has lived in since he was a baby, and rightfully so.

So, how do they deal with this? The truth is: they don't, they don't have to. They have known each other since they were 3 years old and have been attached at the hip ever since. John has never seen Terry as nothing more than his brother, their quarrels have never had nothing to do with their cultural backgrounds. They have eaten multiple times at each other's place and enjoyed the different types of cooking. John travels with Terry to his home-country almost any time he goes.

Did you notice that I have never mentioned this before? It is because there wasn't a real reason to do so: the beauty of exchanging their traditions is beautiful, respectful and, most of all, normal.

It becomes, however, relevant once we understand that, sadly, not every person is respectful and caring with one another as John and Terry are.

They have the "advantage" of having been around one another for as long as possible, for them there's nothing else to it. That's how they grew up, how they have been living for all of their lives.

Some other people didn't come in contact with other cultures other than their own for years, and for that reason, they didn't know how to behave in the face of something that is completely different from their lifestyle.

This can cause many different problems, up to becoming disrespectful and hurting others, while what we should do is be like John and Terry.

Understanding and Respecting Cultural Differences

As previously mentioned, we aren't all like John and Terry: our life experiences are completely different from one another, because we all live different lives. Your neighbor has a whole other perspective on life that is different than yours, even if they had the same upbringing, the same lifestyle, the same age. This happens for many different reasons: the house you grew up in has an influence on certain relationship dynamics. This isn't anyone's merit nor fault, depending on how you look at it: this is just part of our life. We have certain values that our family shares, but as soon as you become a preadolescent, your view on life becomes broader, because you are exposed to many different views. This is when prejudice and curiosity start to arise, that's when you should learn how to become the most open-minded and judgment-free you can.

Try and think of it this way: you wouldn't want someone to criticize you, your upbringing, your family, your traditions, your whole life without even knowing you, would you? That would hurt and could make you feel less of, without having the possibility to defend yourself.

We talked about this when we were discussing traveling and how to be a respectful tourist. We could have also talked about this in the previous chapter, while talking of the many different art forms that exist.

You have a right to be curious, to even be weirded out at first if you come in contact with something that you have never seen before. That's normal. What you should do is to be respectful, always. Respectful of other people's habits, traditions, values, cultures, art forms. "It takes all sorts to make the world", it is so wonderfully diverse! How boring if everyone had one common culture, one way of cooking, one way of celebrating the same holidays. It would become such a dull world.

Also, there isn't room for comparison: there is no such thing as a "better culture", because it would be like comparing egg types. Eggs are eggs, there is no such thing as the best egg. They can come with different colors, shapes and sizes, but they still have yolk and egg white inside of them. You wouldn't throw eggs in the trash just because they aren't exactly the ones you are used to, would you? You have to treat them carefully, otherwise they break, it's almost like you should treat them with...respect! Cultural humility is a crucial learning process that you need to learn and that will help you grow as a loving, respectful person.

Regarding the different art forms: some of them are very different depending from which part of the world you are, or from one's cultural background. Every country has its own history, and the art forms that developed are deeply rooted in this concept. The history of a culture is forever tangled with how a certain art is expressed. There is also a difference between cultural appreciation and appropriation: what makes these two concepts so dissimilar from one another are the intention, the respect you put and your knowledge of that specific culture.

Cultural appreciation: getting in touch with a specific culture, being respectful of it. Embracing it, learning everything about it from the people that live in that culture and have that background. Appreciating it and understanding it. Honoring it. Understanding that you aren't from that culture: if you had a long distant family member that comes from a distant country and lives there, you wouldn't say that you come from there. You wouldn't wear their traditional clothing just because it looks cool to look slightly different. You would, however, have a direct way of learning about that culture, by talking to the family member, visiting them, doing all that we talked about.

Cultural appropriation: this is when you use someone else's culture for your own personal gain. Let's say that you have heard that, in some cultures, they wear a certain type of jewelry. To you, that piece of jewelry is very aesthetically pleasing, so you decide to wear it. You don't know the specifics of why or when it is worn, or worse, you know it, and you choose to ignore it. You aren't appreciating the culture, you're using it as a fashion statement, and that's way disrespectful and rude. If you snapped a picture of a traditional ritual just to gain likes and followers on social media, that would be terrible as well.

It's not hard, you just need to be respectful.

A Broad Perspective of the World

The world doesn't start nor end at the geopolitical borders of your own country: there's an entire world out there, made of cultures and people.

By watching documentaries, studying history, geography, watching videos from all around the world, reading global news, asking questions, you will become aware of how big, wide and full of people the world is.

You could become aware of how other countries are struggling and how you could help, understanding why they are struggling.

You could become fascinated with a far-away country and decide that, one day, you will travel there.

You could also learn that, in order to travel, you need to know some of the stuff before actually taking the plane and landing there: the basics of the language, the etiquette, the currency, how to approach strangers, what's the best way to act in public, how to eat certain traditional dishes or how to eat in general (some countries use cutlery, some chopsticks, some their own hands), how something could be seen as disrespectful in someone's culture and completely acceptable in another (shaking hands, kissing each other on the cheek, bowing to each other are all very different ways of meeting someone).

It's always best to get as much in contact with other cultures other than yours as possible from a young age, so that you can become a full-on citizen of the world in the future!

Diversity and Inclusion

What is diversity: it is accepting that there are many different realities in our universe. To go back to a previous example: eggs can be of a wide variety, but they all have yolk and egg white inside of them. We humans, like eggs, can come from different cultural backgrounds and can have different ethnicities, physical and mental abilities, we can have different gender identities, origins, orientation, family structures, languages, we can be short, tall, with big or small noses... isn't it beautiful? How can we be so different and love and accept each other at the same time? The human experience can be something incredible: it is up to us how we decide to view the world and live in it, but being nice never hurts.

What is inclusion: Imagine that you are in P.E. and you're doing exercises. You then get split into teams to play some sport, but one of your classmates is set aside and has to watch you have fun while they aren't allowed to. They don't know how to include this mate, because they have a physical disability. Your other classmates don't even try to include them. They aren't bullying them, but they surely aren't helping. That's called tolerating, and it's not right. What would you do? The best thing to do would be to go to them and make the sport as inclusive as possible towards that person. There is the possibility that you will play in a different way than usual, but who cares? At least everyone is included, everyone can play. It's not pity, it's not even compassion: decency. Treat others like you would want to be treated, be kind. Involvement is the key to empowerment, it's a win-win situation. It doesn't take too much effort, but the results are amazing.

Conclusion

We have finally arrived at the end of this book, congratulations!

So, there you go, we covered social skills, self-esteem and self-awareness, decision-making and problem-solving, practical skills, preparation for the future, health and wellness, digital skills, creative and artistic skills and cultural and global awareness.

It's ok to feel scared for the future, you are still growing and these are your first big steps into being your own person. You should be proud of yourself, of your previous achievements and the ones you are going to arrive at. You are ready, and if you want, you can always come back to this book, to John, Terry and Max.

You don't have to know everything, nobody knows everything, and I'll let you in on a little secret: even us adults struggle from time to time, even with the things we talked about together.

We are all humans, we are all still growing, even when we are old.

Your priority should always be to be happy and healthy, so keep this information in your pocket, reach out to it whenever you're confused or don't know what to do.

You are strong and resilient, you can achieve everything you want if you put your mind to it.

When you don't feel like it, say these words out loud to yourself, in front of a mirror.

Be sincere with yourself, learn from your mistakes, be kind to yourself and others, try to experience as much as you can but be considerate of your boundaries and of what you are allowed to do.

Be patient, some things take time and for others, you just have to be an adult, and there are reasonable reasons for it.

You have your whole life ahead of you!

John, Terry and Max are always going to be here for you, whenever you need to.

Good luck, you!

I sincerely hope you have enjoyed reading this book on life skills for tweens and that you have found the advice and strategies listed within to be helpful. My hope is that these pieces of information will assist you in building a solid foundation of essential skills needed to successfully navigate the challenges of life during this crucial phase.

If you believe that the book has provided you with valuable knowledge and guidance, I kindly ask you to consider leaving a favorable review. Your positive rating can greatly assist other readers who are seeking helpful resources for tweens. Additionally, it will encourage others to discover and benefit from the advice offered in the book.

Your feedback not only serves as a testament to the effectiveness of the content but also contributes to creating a community where parents and tweens support each other in acquiring important life skills.

Thank you for the time and consideration you put into this request. I wish you and your loved ones ongoing development of vital skills, happiness, and success in future endeavors.

Warmest Regards,

Made in the USA
Las Vegas, NV
15 June 2025